"Mary Poplin takes us on a pilgrimage toward clarity about who we are and what our life amounts to. The pilgrimage is simultaneously through Calcutta and through the heart of the 'sophisticated' dynamics of university life in America. As it proceeds we gain a better understanding of the social forces that govern the university in the name of intellect—but falsely so. It will be of special help to those engaged in academic life, at whatever level. They will find here a guide who has been grasped by God and enabled to see that life and the surrounding cultural world for what they really are, and what under God they could be."

Dallas Willard, professor of philosophy, University of Southern California, and author of *The Divine Conspiracy* and *Hearing God*

"Having been the spiritual director of the Missionaries of Charity in Asia for many years, I read Mary Poplin's book with keen interest and fond memories of these remarkable women. *Finding Calcutta* is a love story between God and two women, Mother Teresa and the author. In describing her encounter and the lessons learned with 'God's pencil,' Mary Poplin has penned 'something beautiful for God.' This book not only captures the spirituality of Mother Teresa and her sisters but also reminds us of an important principle in spiritual formation that God taught its author: our own Calcutta is most often right smack where we are."

Albert Haase, O.F.M., director, School of Spirituality at Mayslake Ministries, and author of *Coming Home to Your True Self: Leaving the Emptiness of False Attractions*

"If you've ever wondered what it would be like to be a worldly California academic curious enough to volunteer in Mother Teresa's Calcutta Mission, prepare to be surprised. After struggling to translate her experience there for a secular audience, Dr. Poplin has ended by translating her readers into Mother Teresa's own unfamiliar, spiritual dimension. Watch out—you will not be able to keep from meditating."

C. John Sommerville, author of *The Decline of the Secular University*

"In this poignant, elegant, humble memoir, Poplin gives us far more than Mother Teresa or even another Mother Teresa story. She gives us instead the Jesus and the Christianity that operated through Mother Teresa. Poplin's experience of finding Calcutta irrevocably changed her soul. It will change yours as well."

Phyllis Tickle, former religion editor, *Publishers Weekly,* and compiler of *The Divine Hours*

"Mary Poplin seeks to integrate her experience with Mother Teresa into her work and life and to come together with others who hunger and thirst. This book can be a platform to gather those of us so disposed so that the flame is not lost and will continue to produce abundant fruit, fruits of eternal life."

Father Angelo Devananda Scolozzi, U.F.W., Centro de Espiritualidad Madre Teresa, Chihuahua, Mexico

"Mary Poplin found her first Calcutta in India as she volunteered in Mother Teresa's ministry to the poorest of the poor. She found her second Calcutta in her own university as she returned to recognize that the poorest of the poor are not always those with no material wealth but those with no knowledge of God and nowhere to find it. The story of her transformed spiritual life segues beautifully into the story of her transformed academic life. An exciting book of great wisdom."

James W. Sire, author of *The Universe Next Door* and *Habits of the Mind*

"A profound journey of the heart, head and hands in which Mary Poplin discovers her own 'Calcutta'—the classroom with its students in whom seeds of life must be sown for the life of the world to come."

Kelly Monroe Kullberg, founder, The Veritas Forum, and author of *Finding God Beyond Harvard: The Quest for Veritas*

"Mary Poplin's pilgrimage of discovering Christ among the most vulnerable of the world's poor is an accessible and inspiring invitation to us all. Her honesty, thoughtfulness and reflections are an important provocation for those who find their realities separated from our sisters and brothers who suffer today. Mary does an excellent job of building the bridges between the insulated and isolated lack of experience of poverty in academia and the oppression and injustice on the streets of one of the world's poorest cities. Her interactions and stories of Mother Teresa and the Missionaries of Charity are a true glimpse of grace and a sweet reminder that God is with and among those who suffer most. Honest, thoughtful and reflective, *Finding Calcutta* will challenge you to love more freely where you find yourself."

Christopher L. Heuertz, international director, Word Made Flesh, and author of *Simple Spirituality: Learning to See God in a Broken World*

"Mary Poplin's spiritually nurturing account of her experiences with the Missionaries of Charity in Calcutta is a loving portrait of a true work of God. In these pages readers encounter Mother Teresa's deep spiritual wisdom as a call to reflection, repentance and a renewed concern for 'the poorest of the poor' as bearers of Christ's image. There is spiritual refreshment here for believer and doubter alike."

James A. Herrick, Guy Vander Jagt Professor of Communication, Hope College, and author of *The Making of the New Spirituality* and *Scientific Mythologies*

FINDING CALCUTTA

What Mother Teresa Taught Me
About Meaningful Work and Service

MARY POPLIN

IVP Books

An imprint of InterVarsity Press
Downers Grove, Illinois

271.97
POPLIN, M

3 1257 01856 7650

InterVarsity Press
P.O. Box 1400, Downers Grove, IL 60515-1426
World Wide Web: www.ivpress.com
E-mail: email@ivpress.com

InterVarsity Press® is the book-publishing division of InterVarsity Christian Fellowship/USA®, a student movement active on campus at hundreds of universities, colleges and schools of nursing in the United States of America, and a member movement of the International Fellowship of Evangelical Students. For information about local and regional activities, write Public Relations Dept., InterVarsity Christian Fellowship/USA, 6400 Schroeder Rd., P.O. Box 7895, Madison, WI 53707-7895, or visit the IVCF website at <www.intervarsity.org>.

Scripture quotations, unless otherwise noted, are from The Holy Bible, English Standard Version, copyright © 2001 by Crossway Bibles, a division of Good News Publishers. Used by permission. All rights reserved.

Excerpts of Mother Teresa's words from Mother Teresa: Come Be My Light, copyright ©2007 Mother Teresa Center. Reprinted with permission. The writings of Mother Teresa of Calcutta are Copyright by the Mother Teresa Center, exclusive licensee throughout the world of the Missionaries of Charity for the works of Mother Teresa.

Design: Cindy Kiple
Images: Mother Teresa: Francois Lochon/Getty Images
       decorative material: iStockphoto

ISBN 978-0-8308-3472-3

Printed in the United States of America ∞

 InterVarsity Press is committed to protecting the environment and to the responsible use of natural resources. As a member of Green Press Initiative we use recycled paper whenever possible. To learn more about the Green Press Initiative, visit <www.greenpressinitiative.org>.

Library of Congress Cataloging-in-Publication Data

Poplin, Mary S., 1951-
  Finding Calcutta: what Mother Teresa taught me about meaningful
  work and service / Mary Poplin.
      p. cm.
  Includes bibliographical references.
  ISBN 978-0-8308-3472-3 (pbk.: alk. paper)
  1. Teresa, Mother, 1910-1997. 2. Work—Religious
aspects—Christianity. 3. Service (Theology) I. Title.
  BX4406.5.Z8P665 2008
  271'.97—dc22
                                                    2008022649

P   23   22   21   20   19   18   17   16   15   14   13   12   11   10   9   8   7   6   5   4   3   2

Y   27   26   25   24   23   22   21   20   19   18   17   16   15   14   13   12   11   10   09   08

Finally, brethren, whatsoever things are true,

whatsoever things are honest, whatsoever things are just,

whatsoever things are pure, whatsoever things are lovely,

whatsoever things are of good report; if there be any virtue,

and if there be any praise, think on these things.

Philippians 4:8 KJV

In memory of Mother Teresa,

whose life eternally renders glory to God.

In honor of the Missionaries of Charity,

who follow every day in her footsteps, serving Christ

in the "distressing disguise of the poor."

And

In honor of my parents, George and Inez Poplin,

for the extraordinary and countless number of

"small things done with great love."

Contents

Introduction

Telling the Truth About Mother Teresa

IN THE SPRING OF 1996, I WENT TO CALCUTTA to work
for about two months as a volunteer with Mother Teresa and the
Missionaries of Charity. Mother Teresa was eighty-six years old;
I was forty-four. It was about a year and a half before her death in
September 1997. Two years prior, I was at a monastery in Pecos,
New Mexico, when I saw an excellent film by Ann and Jeanette
Petrie in which a group had followed and filmed Mother Teresa
for five years.[1] Before this, I had not given the work of this small,
curious-looking nun much thought, but the film touched me in a
way I could not explain. The very force of her work and her life
had an inexplicable effect on me.

After that, I found a number of books that were collections
of her letters, speeches and interviews; and a book by Malcolm
Muggeridge that had been significant in introducing her to the

West.[2] One thing Mother Teresa repeatedly said was that their work was religious work, not social work. I found this statement intriguing and wanted to know what she meant. What could those of us who live and work outside a religious order learn from her religious work?

Therefore I sent a letter to the Mother House in Calcutta in the fall of 1995 asking if I could volunteer during my upcoming spring sabbatical from the private graduate university where I work. For months I received no answer and then, the week before my sabbatical began, a letter arrived saying that I could come. I had asked what to bring to Calcutta. The letter from Sister Priscilla, who was in charge of volunteers, answered, "Come with a heart to love and hands to serve Jesus in the crippled, the abandoned, the sick and dying in any one of our centres."

While this response quickened my spirit, my "soulish" mind did something else with it. All of my years of secular education and experience—still very much alive in me—fought with the phrase "to serve Jesus." Surely I had volunteered to serve people. I had just begun to encounter people who talked about Jesus as a living person, someone with whom they had a relationship. While I had attended Sunday school in a liberal Protestant church somewhat regularly during my childhood due to my father's faithfulness, I had for many years walked far from God. In fact, if the truth were told, I had become quite hostile to what I thought was Christianity. I had tried almost everything to fill the void I unconsciously sensed.

The void and the search to fill it took many forms. First, I was never sure what I was supposed to do in the world. Was I falling into jobs, relationships and philosophies of life randomly? Was I going anywhere or getting anything done? Could I ever contribute? Somehow I was certain that everyone is supposed to contribute something, but I was confused. What exactly was my purpose for being on this planet? I filled my life with lots of activities, but perhaps this was to avoid the serious questions which I felt had no answers. Second, I was certain that spiritual reality did exist, but I had accepted what many intellectuals believe: that Christianity is not where progressives go for "spiritual action." Therefore, to fill the void spiritually, I dabbled in feminist theology, various Eastern religions and forms of meditation, drugs, and the New Age movement in its multiple forms.

Intellectually the void was filled by constantly learning, accepting and teaching a wide range of contemporary philosophies and theories as they applied to education. Indeed, I had also come to believe and teach what my fellow leftist intellectual and radical feminist friends believed—that Christianity was oppressive, the root of most social ills in the world. Of course it never occurred to me to raise my head above my radical texts to notice that the places founded on Christianity just happen to be where people are the least oppressed. I also had tested most of what the world has to offer in the way of lifestyles and methods of entertainment and escape. I was, as the song proclaims, "looking for love in all the wrong places."

In January 1993, I did what I never imagined I would ever do: I opened my life to Christ. It began with an unshakeable dream, followed by a friend's counsel, and ended (or rather began) with a prayer that was more of a timid request said with considerable measures of resignation, hope and doubt. Much to my surprise, at age forty-one, I knelt down at a communion rail in a tiny Methodist church in Glen Alpine, North Carolina, where my mother had grown up, and said to Jesus, "If you are real, please come and get me." And he did. I began the lifelong journey of pursuing his presence in my life, trying—albeit clumsily—to follow him. Yet even my newfound commitment to Christ had not prepared me for what I was about to experience at Mother Teresa's. I should

have been able to foresee this in my uneasy response to the name
of Jesus in the letter.

I tell you this before I begin the story about Mother Teresa and
the Missionaries because I believe I am not alone in my struggles
to understand the truth of her life and work—struggles born of
living in a secular age. I can see now that even the church in which
I grew up taught more about being a "good humanist" than about
living with and for Christ. For the first few years after my return from India, I attempted to write this book in a way I thought
would appeal to everyone. Even though I did not personally seek
a secular interpretation, I felt that only such a description of her
would resonate with our culture and time. After repeatedly starting to write and then laying it aside for long periods, I finally realized: one cannot understand or explain Mother Teresa in secular
terms. Indeed that is precisely what she meant when she said,
"Our work is not social work; it is religious work."

My struggle to write this book, to tell the truth about Mother
Teresa, and my struggles in the university are a testimony both to
a lost public conversation and to a worldview that is very difficult
for many in Western culture to comprehend fully, even some of
us who profess Christ. As one colleague put it in a recent discussion about Mother Teresa's "dark nights," she was like a medieval
Christian, which says as much about our current Christian con-
victions and understandings as about her otherworldliness. She
lived her faith more like the mystics who lived in ancient monasteries, believing in penance, daily communion, and a strictly
disciplined life of prayer and work. Yet, here she was in the center
of one of the world's most chaotic urban cities.

Mother Teresa was not interested in universities, philosophies,
worldviews or public conversations. She was not an intellectual,
and yet she had a profound understanding of the Christian life.
More astonishingly, she lived it; there was no guile in her. As an

intellectual, I have often convinced myself that I am living something just because I think I understand it.

She was not simply a good humanitarian. When I tried to write about her in this way, I had to concentrate on her work, but dismiss the power of God that brought it into being and sustained her. Rather, she was a devout, simple, strong and sacrificial woman who fully belonged to Jesus. She told us she was called by God (she did not decide on her own) to go into "the dark holes of the poorest of the poor" to do small things with great love in order to bring Christ to the poorest and the poorest to Christ.

Mother Teresa was like a prophet crying in the wilderness, revealing all at once my poverty, my wretchedness and my possibilities. Abraham Heschel once wrote that true prophets of God "ceaselessly shatter indifference."[3] He believed they reveal the heart of God, imploring us to return to him in "a world that is not so much devoid of meaning as deaf to meaning." That was Mother Teresa's life. To see her and the Missionaries serving the poor and living among them simultaneously shatters our indifference to God and humanity, critiques our privilege and disturbs our comfort. This was not what she consciously set out to do. As Heschel pointed out, prophets are often reluctant messengers that simply allow God to speak through them. All prophets and apostles suffer, and Mother Teresa was not immune to this. She said our suffering was nothing compared to Jesus' who suffered the ultimate sacrifice to achieve our freedom. The supreme injustice is that the perfect man/God was crucified to redeem the world.

In this book I am not trying to convince anyone that Mother Teresa or the Missionaries are perfect. I am certain they have "bad" days (though never a bad hair day). She said herself that the greatest hindrance to their work was that they were not yet saints, not fully able to spread the full love of Christ because of their human weaknesses. Neither is this a biography; others more capable have written those.[4] Since I cannot write about Mother Teresa from a secular point of view without distorting who she was in Christ, I will leave it to the readers of other religious or secular faiths to translate the stories for themselves.

This, then, is the simple story of my brief encounter with Mother Teresa and the Missionaries of Charity and of my struggles then and now to understand—and more importantly, to live—the lessons in our culture and times. It is an ongoing tale of how I listen to God through her life and through the lives of others who graciously serve as guides to me. It is the story of how God used her and the Missionaries to cause a crisis in my own life which revealed more clearly my purpose and my calling.

Mother called it "finding your Calcutta."*

---

*In January of 2000, the name of Calcutta was changed to Kolkata. I use Calcutta in the text because all my experiences and Mother Teresa's life were lived prior to this, and it would be inaccurate to use Kolkata in quotes from her.

I

Getting There

W HEN I WROTE TO MOTHER TERESA and the Missionaries
of Charity asking if I could come and work for a couple of months,
I did not have in mind "Do[ing] Something Beautiful for God." Yet
this is the message that hung above the doorway to the children's
center where I would eventually be assigned. In all honesty, I was
thinking of doing something for myself that had more or less to do
with serving the poor and with my relationship with God. It was
not for some beautiful or holy reason that I was going to Calcutta.
Indeed I harbored no thoughts that they needed my help or that I
would even be particularly helpful. I wanted to know why Mother
Teresa said her work was not social work but religious work. She
said repeatedly that they do not run hospitals or schools but "religious centers."

When by mid-December I still had no reply, I felt discouraged.
Other opportunities waited in the wings for sabbatical. I had been
invited to do a series of lectures in Great Britain, and a friend

wanted me to study with her in Jerusalem, but my heart was set on Calcutta. I knew it was very likely that the Missionaries did not want another volunteer or would write and tell me to volunteer in my own city, as I had heard they sometimes did. As I mailed the letter, I prayed that God's will would prevail because that is what a Christian is supposed to do. However, I was not yet three years following Christ and did not really understand the seriousness of this principle yet. In prayer I committed my desires into God's hands. My emotions did not necessarily agree. I wanted to go despite the fact that I had hardly set foot outside the United States and had certainly never traveled anywhere as foreign to me as India.

Arriving home late after teaching the last class of the semester, I reached in the mailbox and pulled out a tattered, once-pink-now-yellowed envelope. The return address was Calcutta. The letter, postmarked New York City, was lined with ten- and one-cent stamps. I was later to learn that traveling sisters and returning volunteers often took mail to foreign countries to lessen the expense of overseas postage. I immediately opened the fragile envelop to discover inside a small, mismatched, white piece of paper obviously typed on an old manual typewriter. The message began, "Thank you very much for your letter. You are welcome to share in our works of love for the poorest of the poor."

My heart, which only a few moments before had been heavy, was now as light as air. My sabbatical was set. In an instant I began making plans in my mind. I would leave for Calcutta in March after finishing a writing project, and stay until May. Then I would join my good friend, Geralyn, a Benedictine sister, at the end of her studies in Jerusalem, and we would travel with her classmates on the route that Paul had taken through Turkey and Greece. She and I would continue to visit various places important to each of us on the way home. First, I had to know what Mother

Teresa meant when she said her work was not social work but religious work.

Through a series of divine interventions, the trip came together effortlessly. First, Marjorie, an alumnus and friend who grew up in India, called to wish me a Merry Christmas. I had lost touch with her when she moved to northern California. She told me she was on her way to see her family in India for Christmas. When I told her I was going to Calcutta, she immediately volunteered that I should come and stay with her and her husband as soon as she returned, and they would take me to the Indian consulate in San Francisco to apply for my visa. She sent me a list of all the paperwork I would need. We completed the whole process in January in the time it took to drive into the city, drop off the forms and enjoy lunch on the beach while we waited.

Marjorie also told me about her friend Neepa from Calcutta living near me that I should call. I did and was invited over for tea. That afternoon while Marjorie's friend showed me books on Calcutta and introduced me to masala tea, a couple also from Calcutta, Mitra and Swapan, dropped by. The man had a cell phone long before they were common. He asked to see the information the Missionaries had sent me regarding places to stay, and the date and time of my arrival. At that very moment, he called a friend living in Calcutta—Goudi, an accomplished architect. Goudi told him she would meet me at the airport and that I could stay with her for a few days until I found a place to live. Things were coming together with very little effort on my part.

On the Friday before I left, I visited a friend who is a Korean acupressurist, Syng Yu. We talked about the trip, and he told me of his adventures in India. Before I left, he reached into a closet and handed me a roll of Indian bills left over from a trip years before. I had no idea how much money he had given me, but I was grateful.

On Sunday before my Monday departure, I knelt in church and looked up at the larger-than-life crucifix over the altar. I was nervous about the trip, and in my spirit I felt the Lord say, "Now it is just between you and me." I wondered if my newfound faith would sustain me.

On Monday, the terminal in Los Angeles was chaotic. There was no Indian money at the currency office, but they assured me there would be plenty in London. The plane departed over an hour late. My connection in London to a Delhi-bound flight was tight; there was nothing to do but pray. (I thought of prayer like this, though now I see it must be very offensive to God, as though his power is only a last resort. Nevertheless, he is very merciful to his children—especially his little new ones.) As the flight continued, I began to read my Bible. An Englishman approached and said, "You don't often see people on airplanes reading a Bible. Tell me about yourself." I told him I was a new Christian and was on my way to work with Mother Teresa and the Missionaries. He said he was part of World Vision and that he and his wife once had been to see Mother Teresa. He told me they would pray for me; I was grateful.

As the plane finally landed in London, we learned from the cabin crew that there would be additional security measures prior to our next flights. I looked at my watch and realized my plane for Delhi was about to leave. As I waited in the packed aisle of this enormous plane, an airline employee began paging, "Would Mr. Poplin please identify himself at the door." Despite the mix up on gender, I assumed they meant me. When I got to the door, I identified myself. They whisked me off to a waiting airport cart. I flew through security checkpoints with the airline agents clearing the way. At last I boarded the plane and we left. I was tremendously relieved and knew I was the recipient of great grace and favor. Once again, I had not had the opportunity to exchange money.

I arrived in Delhi after ten in the evening. Although I had a reservation at a hotel, I did not know how far it was from the airport. My travel agent had told me to take a cab and that I would need Indian currency, but the currency exchange was closed. I was hoping that I had enough in the wad of bills Syng Yu had given me. I found I had plenty; in fact, the money totaled over one hundred U.S. dollars—more grace. I slept and woke early enough for breakfast in this land of new sights, sounds and smells.

As the flight took off for Calcutta, I began to wonder if this stranger really would show up to greet me and take me into her home. One would think that by now my faith had risen; and it had. However, for new Christians, sheer faith in unknown situations is a precious but fragile jewel, always held with great amazement, yet tentativeness, as though one may awake and find the grace suddenly gone. I think at first we assume grace means having our own plans fulfilled and feeling good, rather than that grace is also the propeller for growth. Sometimes this means not having our plans fulfilled and not feeling good. Real trust in God, I was later to learn, demands faith in both situations.

As I emerged from customs on Tuesday morning, there were Goudi and her friend holding a sign with my name on it. By the end of the first day, we were rapidly becoming good friends, and she volunteered that I rent her extra room. Her flat was only a twenty-minute walk from the Mother House where I would begin work each day with Mass and prayers.

The sights, smells and sounds of Calcutta took some getting used to. It seemed that everyone who drove a car honked incessantly. The smells were not just aromas of new cuisine (which I quite enjoyed) but of rotting garbage, the refuse of cows considered holy and people living on the streets. I was clearly in a foreign land, yet I began to feel completely safe in the arms of a God I scarcely knew.

2

A Day in the Life
of a Missionary of Charity

I ARRIVED IN CALCUTTA ON TUESDAY, and on Thursday, I walked
in to report for volunteer duty, naively thinking I had come to
answer a simple and somewhat academic question. Inside the
Mother House, a tremendous sense of peace filled the space in
sharp contrast to the chaotic street. The Mother House was where
Mother—as she is always called here—lived with a group of finally
professed sisters (those who had taken final vows that at that time
took nine years) and a larger group of novice sisters. The admin-
istrative work of the Missionaries of Charity is largely conducted
here. Inside a small room off the dining area, Sister Bethany and a
volunteer were speaking with newly arrived volunteers.

I immediately discovered that the Missionaries ran many centers in Calcutta alone—including a home for the dying, two children's homes, two homes for disabled adults who were not able
to live alone and many others. Sisters lived at each of the other

centers. I volunteered to go wherever I was most needed, assuming it would be with the adults at Nirmal Hriday (Pure Heart), the Home for the Dying. However, Sister Bethany told me they had many volunteers for adults at that time and few for children. Would I please go down the street to Shishu Bhavan (Children's Home), to help with the sick and handicapped children there? Unbeknownst to them, I had begun my career teaching handicapped children. I agreed and was given a little handwritten assignment card and instructions to report the next morning after Mass to Dana, the volunteer in charge of volunteers for that center. Dana had served in Calcutta for about nine months while on a year's leave from teaching in inner-city Chicago. She was one of the most faithful volunteers.

The first few days, I took a cab from Goudi's flat. I soon discovered that the route to the Mother House was quite simple and began to memorize it. A cab strike the second week set me to walking probably before I would have otherwise. It was just turning light when I would start out at about 5:20 a.m. Sleeping people littered the street; some were just rising and bathing at public water spigots. Goats followed their owners who stopped by residences and businesses to deliver fresh milk.

By the time I reached the Mother House each morning, the sisters had already had early prayers and begun the chores of cooking and preparing for the day. They had also washed and hung to dry the saris worn the day before by drawing water in buckets from a single spigot in the courtyard and beating the saris on the pavement. At 5:50, we all met together in the chapel for Mass, the official beginning of our day.

The chapel was a long, rectangular room with a concrete floor on the second story of the Mother House. It was sparse, like everything else. We took off our shoes before entering and sat or knelt on the floor like the Missionaries. The back, right section was reserved for volunteers and visitors. Two small, woven stools in the middle section of the back were for Mother Teresa and some of the older sisters to sit on, except when kneeling. A couple of benches behind the volunteers allowed guests to sit if needed. The chapel contained no other chairs or benches. My weak Protestant-raised knees became Catholic quickly; we knelt much more than is typical in Catholic churches in the United States, and kneeling cushions were nowhere to be found.

A crucifix hung in the middle of the long wall that faced onto the street. The words "I thirst" were written over it. Even at 6:00 a.m., Calcutta traffic was heavy and noisy, and the chapel's ancient public address system of little effect. A statue of Mary stood off to the right. Fresh, handpicked flowers graced the altar area. Two chairs behind the altar and to its left were reserved for priests from all over the world who presided on different days. English is the official language which unites the Missionaries around the globe. Yet they also speak the languages of the people they serve in each location. Additional prayers recited before and after Mass were typed on a card, a copy of which we were given as a gift when we left. A board outside the chapel announced prayer requests for ill families, sisters abroad and other special requests.

Mother Teresa often urged volunteers to come to Mass and special sessions led by a priest one evening a week. We also could attend Adoration, an hour of prayer, in the evenings between six and seven o'clock. I attended Mass almost every day and Adoration on occasion. After Mass, Mother Teresa frequently spoke with us and handed out religious medals, rosaries and especially little cards with prayers on them—Mother called them her "business cards." I still have my turquoise and black plastic rosary she handed me one day and a number of her "business cards." A small but constant stream of visitors appeared at Mass and the centers.

There were some days when for no explainable reason and without thinking, we spontaneously lowered our heads as Mother Teresa passed. On these days, she would touch our heads lightly and bless us. Her black eyes were intense and undistracted when she spoke to you. I wondered if in her later years, when she was less able to do the hard labor at the various centers, she increased her attention on the volunteers. I would often see her during Mass look out over our motley group and bury her head in her hands to pray.

Following Mass, we ate a small breakfast of a slice of bread, a tiny tropical banana and a cup of hot tea. Then, at seven, the Missionaries spilled out into the streets two-by-two or four-by-four to go to various parts of the city. They carried plastic bottles of water recycled and refilled after collecting them from the volunteers. We followed them to the centers we had been assigned. Even in the short blocks I had to walk from the Mother House to Shishu Bhavan, I noticed that the Missionaries were not always appreciated. Most of the time people simply stared at them as oddities; occasionally someone would insult them by word or expression. A man in whose store many of the volunteers bought water would tell us that "they should let those people die. India has too many people." The Missionaries gently ignored the insults, choosing instead to smile, fold their hands and bow their heads in a gesture of blessing. Some people would timidly return the greeting.

Every morning additional, temporary centers sprang up in streets all over Calcutta. The lack of a building did not deter the Missionaries from serving where needs were greatest. Sisters would carry heavy bags filled with supplies. Several sisters in a moment could turn a street corner into a medical or food dispensary, or a school for children. They taught by drawing in the dirt if necessary. The "schools" were not really schools; they existed only to prepare children for school. They were daytime places of refuge and joy for street children. Mother said of them,

They are nothing, they are just little primary schools where
we teach the children to love the school and to be clean and
so on—if we didn't have these little schools, those children,
those thousands of children would be left in the streets. So
we have to choose either to take them and give them just a
little or leave them in the street.[1]

Upon arriving at Shishu, a man opened the compound doors
to inquire of the visitor's intent. I walked in easily beside Dana
who was now well-known. A couple of ambulances were parked
just inside the gates, donated by groups around the world to take
children to the hospital or doctor, or to carry the infirm or dying
on the streets to the appropriate center. Across the front of the
largest building in the complex where children for adoption live
was a large sign: Do Something Beautiful for God. This was one
of Mother's favorite expressions. To the right was a large, covered
patio where the hungry from the streets were fed, and a medical
dispensary was set up each day.

The three-story building above this patio is where I spent most
of my time. The ground floor contained rooms for an office and
medical supply storage; children with tuberculosis lived on the
second floor; and children with other illnesses and handicaps
lived in the large room at the top. We left our shoes outside and
took plaid aprons from the hooks. Forty to fifty children ranging
in age from newborns to ten-year-olds lived in this top room. It
was bright and sunny and always very warm despite the work of
ceiling fans, but the children seemed not to notice. They greeted
us by calling us "auntie." The older and more verbal children
would often try a few foreign words on us. *Bonjour* and *hello* were
frequent favorites. They giggled at our responses. Giggling was
the universal language since so few volunteers spoke any Bengali.
Most of the children were Muslim, though Calcutta is about half

Hindu and half Muslim. It is estimated that slightly over 2 percent of Indians are Christian.[2]

The children and infants had various handicaps and illnesses ranging from serious deformities to mild forms of retardation. The illnesses varied from intestinal viruses to malaria, hepatitis, tuberculosis and other diseases. Sometimes we nursed children who were ill and not for adoption; we simply kept them until they recovered. Other times, we cared for healthy babies whose parents were ill. Whatever the need, there was always a way to meet it and always enough room for one more.

Off to one side of the large room was a laundry area with showers and bathrooms for the children. Laundry, done by hand in large tubs, was endless; the soiled, plaid, cotton diapers multiplied before your eyes, like autumn leaves while you rake them. Another crude bathroom (by Western standards)[3] served the adults, and a staircase led to the roof where older children sometimes played with volunteers. Next to the laundry and bathroom was another small room for food distribution, and on the other side of the same wall was a room for preparing infant formulas.

At one end of the spacious room were infants in bassinets and at the other end, large cribs and youth beds for older children. A space along the wall facing the street provided the children a place to play. At the infants' end were wooden benches under more windows where we sat to feed them. The older and ambulatory children roved through the room playing their made-up games. Their jovial antics went unnoticed by sleeping infants who were accustomed to the noise of Calcutta.

No air conditioning relieved the heat in the centers because of the Missionaries' commitment to living like the poor. The only place I saw fans was the children's home. The temperature outside rose above 110 degrees Fahrenheit; I doubt it ever fell below 100 during the day while I was there. The children and Missionaries seemed unaffected. Nights offered little relief from the sweltering heat and oppressive humidity. I read that Calcutta has the most serious air, water and sound pollution of any city in the world. The depth and breadth of poverty in Calcutta is difficult to describe. The lack of sanitation for those who live on the streets, and the cows and other animals that roam freely, creates even more problems.

Volunteers worked every day except Thursdays. On this day the novices ran the centers while the other sisters took care of business, confession, reconciliation, inducting new volunteers and extra prayer. Except a few days when suffering with a cold or stomach flu, I worked six days a week. I would feed, wash clothes, clean, change diapers and play with the children. I was assigned most "tall" cleaning tasks because at five foot eight inches, I towered above most of the sisters. Since many of the volunteers were very young and not as comfortable with babies, I soon found myself primarily working with sick infants while the younger volunteers helped keep the older, handicapped children fed and entertained with imaginative, spontaneous games.

Most of the volunteers were young, in their twenties, and came from all over the world. While I was there, the majority were from Europe, followed by Asia and North America; fewer were from Africa and South America. Frankly, some volunteers needed more care than they were capable of giving, and they were not always dependable. There were a few days when only two or three of us showed up at Shishu Bhavan. Many of the young volunteers arrived in India in search of ashrams, temples, mosques, meditation centers and even the small street vendors with charms, spiritual advice and tattoos. Mother Teresa was just one stop on their journey. They were often taking a year off college or deciding whether to go to college, searching for what to try next. They had come primarily to "find themselves" and secondarily to "help others." I often just listened to their conversations over breakfast.

Some of these young volunteers seemed lost in a world that offered them more choices than direction. They wanted to be countercultural, but did not know why or how. They wanted to believe that all religions make people good, and they desperately wanted to be good. They often described themselves as "spiritual but not religious." I believe Mother Teresa drew them because they already had become disillusioned with the world, and their lives felt uncertain and meaningless. She was someone who knew her purpose in life. They admired her work but had little understanding or teaching about the Christ that led and sustained her. Some ignored her talk of Jesus and pleas to attend Mass, chalking it up to an old woman who did not understand their world. They were unaware that this was the most important thing they could learn from her. Her simplicity, certainty, notoriety and commitment to the poor drew them. Dana, the teacher from Chicago, was one of the few volunteers I met who was there largely because of her commitment to Christ. She was an evangelical Protestant. There must have been others, but they were the exception and not the rule.

It was painful for me to see the young seekers as they mirrored my not-so-distant past. I knew the indefinable pain they suffered—the uncertainty, the constant moving from one thing to another in hopes of finding a formula that would make them feel and be good. I knew some found Mass boring. I knew some were wandering while they rebelled against their parents (yet depended on their parents' money). They, like me, had come to distrust all authority, not yet realizing that authority, like anything else, can be good or evil. I also had gone in search of what I believed were more exotic or intellectual religions because I did not understand the depth of Christianity. To be honest, I avoided Christianity because I knew that if Christ were real, he would not have approved of my life and I would have to change. It was much later that I realized his disapproval was really because he wanted so much more for me.

I also observed that those of us volunteers from the more technologically developed nations were physically weaker. We were much more prone to catching colds and stomach viruses, and much less able to maintain our vigor in the humid heat. We were used to air conditioning, antibiotics, antibacterial soaps and purified water.

Other men and women from poor communities also worked alongside the Missionaries as paid helpers. The children called them Mashi, which means "aunt" in Bengali. They performed incredible amounts of work at the centers. Some were committed Catholics and very faithful to that work as well.

Our shift lasted from early morning until after the children had finished their lunch. We helped feed the infants and children their breakfast, lunch and a midmorning snack, usually fresh fruit. The lunch was generally rice, vegetables and dal (a mixture like lentil soup). Occasionally we had boiled eggs to crumble over the food. We fed, changed and played with the children, and helped the Missionaries and Mashis with daily tasks. After lunch, the children rested in their beds or on large mats on the floor. Then it was time for us to go. Another group of volunteers would arrive in a couple of hours and work from three to six. Such was the day of a volunteer.

Back at Goudi's home, I would eat a delicious vegetarian lunch prepared by the servants. It was disconcerting that I was not allowed to do the work I did at Mother Teresa's, and even in my own home—here it was the work of servants. Though I washed children's clothes in the morning, I was not allowed to wash my own in the afternoon. After lunch I would take notes in a journal or study the Scriptures and other books about Mother Teresa that I found in Calcutta. Occasionally I also would read English storybooks or work mathematics with the young boy of the house. He was the son of one of the servants and was being sent by Goudi to the private schools where she had sent her own sons. I often fell into naps during the hottest part of the afternoon. For the Missionaries, their schedule continued.

At 12:30, the Missionaries ate lunch and did their own housework. Then for a half an hour, every sister rested, followed by a time for examination of conscience and prayers. At 2:00, they had spiritual reading for half an hour and then tea before going back to work from three to six. Adoration was from 6:00 to 7:00, at 7:30 dinner and then a few minutes to prepare for the next day.[4] From 8:30 to 9:00 was recreation and time to visit one another. Night prayers were said at 9:00.

It was after night prayers on September 5, 1997, that Mother Teresa said goodnight to the sisters and to Jesus. Then falling on her cot, she took her last breath. The sisters tried to revive her with a breathing machine, but at that moment both of the two independent electric supplies in the Mother House went out.[5] She worked full days to the very end, arising in the middle of the night to answer letters and write to the sisters.

Such is a typical day in the life of a Missionary of Charity "doing something beautiful for God."[6]

3

A Pencil in God's Hand

≫⊰≪

I ALWAYS TRIED TO GET TO MASS A LITTLE EARLY SO I could sit near Mother Teresa's stool. I think I was hoping that some of her spirit would rub off on me. One morning during Mass, a well-dressed Indian woman rushed in and threw herself at Mother's feet. She began to bow to her and kiss her hands and feet. Mother Teresa's face became stern and she pointed to the crucifix on the wall directly across the room. At first I thought she was motioning that the Mass was in session and that the woman should be more reverent. But the woman continued her adulation. Then I saw Mother take the woman's hands in hers and point them to the crucifix. She said something in a language I did not understand and then firmly in English, "It is not me, it is him. Give your thanks to him." The woman stopped, looked up, looked at Mother, looked at the cross, sat still for several minutes and then left.

Mother Teresa often referred to herself as "a pencil in God's hand." She believed that everything she was able to do was done by

God's power working through her. Many people perceive Mother Teresa as someone who looked out at the poor and responded to their suffering with her own kindness, love and energy. This is not at all how Mother saw her calling. When anyone complimented Mother, she would always say, "It is him, his work." She meant this literally—God did the work through her.

For most of the twenty years prior to her work with the poor, Mother Teresa taught at a wealthy girl's school in Calcutta run by the sisters of Our Lady of Loreto, an order she had joined at eighteen. On September 10, 1946, at the age of 36, during a train ride to Darjeeling for her annual retreat, she heard the voice of Jesus calling her to leave the order and gather Indian sisters who would radiate his love to the poorest of the poor, the sick, the dying and the street children. This same voice repeated itself over the next several months. Mother rarely spoke of these experiences except to a few confessors and direct superiors.[1] After almost two years of working with her superiors and various ecclesiastical authorities, she successfully acquired permission to leave the order and work in the streets. On August 17, 1948, she set out alone with five rupees to receive medical training. On December 21 of that same year, she walked into the slums. It was not until October 7, 1950, that the Missionaries of Charity were officially established.

She wrote in her journal about her first day on the streets in December 1948:

> What dirt and misery—what poverty and suffering.—I spoke very, very little, I just did some washing of sores, and dressings, gave medicine to some.—The old man lying on the street—not wanted—all alone just sick and dying—I gave him carborsone and water to drink and the old man was so strangely grateful. . . . Then we went to Taltala Ba-

zaar, and there was a very poor woman dying I think of starvation more than TB. What poverty. What actual suffering. I gave something that will help her to sleep—but the woman longs to have some care . . . confession and holy Communion.—I felt my own poverty there too—for I had nothing to give that poor woman—I did everything I could but if I had been able to give her a hot cup of milk or something like that, her cold body would have got some life—I must try and be somewhere close to the people where I could easily get at things.[2]

Once when a reporter asked Mother to describe her life, she began with her childhood in Skopje, Albania. Then she explained her move to join the Loreto sisters in Ireland, her transition to India a year later and her life as a sister of Loreto. As she related the shift to serve the poor, she stopped and said, "And that was the end of my life." Muggeridge says, "It was the end of her biography and the beginning of her life."[3]

She believed the Missionaries were only able to do the work they do by the power, love and mercy of God. I came to understand why this must be true. Most social workers—like me in my early adult years—move in and out of private middle class lives to serve the poor, generally receiving payment for the work. By contrast, the Missionaries live the lives of the poor. Their everyday routine is feeding, cleaning and tending the sick, the dying, and the poorest of the poor—with no salary. No abstract system of food stamps or special programs supplement their efforts. To me, the work would have soon become boring, physically grueling and even discouraging, but not for them. Mother Teresa said, "A Christian is a tabernacle of the living God." That is the way they saw their work—as him "dwelling in them."[4] She also said, "I wouldn't touch a leper for a thousand pounds; yet I willingly care for him for the love of God."[5]

Father John Bettuolucci alludes to the distinction between social work and religious work when he writes:

> Social action without prayer and conversion to the Lord lacks power and the ability to produce long-lasting change in the socio-economic conditions of the poor. Likewise prayer and evangelism without social action leads to pietistic withdrawal from the realities of the human condition and an escape from social problems rather than a confrontation and challenge to change.[6]

I thought of how differently I frame my life than these sisters even though I am a Christian. I forget that God wants to make his home with me, direct my steps and give me his power to do his will. I often think I chose my own work by my good sense and careful control of circumstances, rather than that God formed me for specific purposes. I flatter myself that it is out of my own goodness that I do things for others. Nevertheless, when I am most honest, I confess that many of the "good" things I do are really as much or more for me than for those to whom they are given. I find it hard to live out what the apostle Paul said, "It is no longer I who live, but Christ who lives in me."[7]

Yet Mother's life reveals that the more yielded we are to God, the more clearly we will grasp our calling. The more we empty our focus on ourselves, the more he can fill us. Mother Teresa said that "humility is nothing but the truth"[8] and that accepting humiliation is "the surest way to be one with God . . . Humiliation because we know we have nothing in ourselves. You see what God has done. I think God is wanting to show His greatness by using our nothingness."[9] Bernard of Clairvaux in the twelfth century wrote, "Humility is that virtue by which a man has a low opinion of himself because he knows himself well."[10]

I have come to understand that my lack of humility limits my life. My pride not only gives me the illusion that I am the master of my fate, but it also causes me to limit what I will attempt. Knowing my natural limitations, I narrow my work accordingly. Yet Mother saw her "nothingness" and God's greatness, and in due course established a worldwide organization. She could say with Paul, "For this I toil, struggling with all his energy that he powerfully works within me."[11]

Mother Teresa's journey with Christ was a rigorous one that required a deep awareness of her own human frailty. One of her most fervent, lifelong prayers was that she would never say no to Jesus. Today her order, one of the most demanding in the Catholic church, is also one of the most vigorous. For the many that hunger for a disciplined, just and righteous life, Mother and the Missionaries demonstrate that such a life is possible.

This rigor requires availability twenty-four hours a day, seven days a week. A ricksha puller once said,

> I married very late and I have four small children. Sometimes when I am not able to collect my rations, I have to beg for a few rupees. If I don't get anything, my children would starve that night. But I know that if I knock on these doors even in the middle of the night, no Sister will send me away without a little something. Sometimes it is only a packet of biscuits and milk for the children but that night we don't go hungry.[12]

I never heard a Missionary of Charity say that she could not do something. Some mornings, two or three more children would appear at the center having arrived during the night. I wondered if I had slept there, would I have been willing to rise to answer the door.

No matter the hour, when the poor came to the Missionaries, they were met by one of God's pencils positioned in his hand ready to write.

4

Whatever You Did for the
Least of These, You Did for Me

OCCASIONALLY MOTHER TERESA TAUGHT the volunteers and visitors a Scripture by using her five fingers. She pointed to each one and said emphatically, "You–did–it–for–me ." In the book of Matthew, Christ tells his disciples, "I was hungry and you gave me food, I was thirsty and you gave me drink, I was a stranger and you welcomed me, I was naked and you clothed me, I was sick and you visited me, I was in prison and you came to me." The disciples ask when they ever saw Jesus in these conditions. Jesus answers, "Truly, I say to you, as you did it to one of the least of these my brothers, you did it to me."[1]

This is one of the primary Scriptures that informs the work of the Missionaries. Their faith in it causes them to see everyone as Christ—the starved old man on the street, half eaten by worms and rats; the deformed infant in a garbage heap; the young volunteer without direction in life; or a tourist satisfying his curiosity.

When people showed up at the door, Mother believed that whether they knew it or not, they were not really coming to encounter her, but Christ.

Someone once told me about a woman who had gone to Calcutta to "get to know" Mother Teresa and found her impersonal. I often laugh when people talk about her as though she were some sweet, old grandmother. I would never characterize Mother as either impersonal or sweet; rather, she was strong and sacrificial. Aside from the fact that Mother Teresa's calling was not about tending to volunteers, she did not need to get to know us. Once we arrived, we did not need to build a relationship with Mother and the Missionaries, because they assumed we already had a relationship with them, because God had sent us. Thus she trusted that he would see to it that we received what we needed through our experiences there.

On the other hand, most of us build relationships through a kind of elaborate, systematic exchange of stories. I tell you my stories, you tell me yours; and during the time we are together we constantly make determinations about how much to tell and how much to withhold. Through this ritual, we choose who will be our friends and who will not. However, she did not see herself as having this choice or needing to form that kind of personal relationship. She assumed a bond between us that went through God. Rather than construct a horizontal relationship between humans, she understood relationships more as a triangle with God at the top. I do not think in the entire two months I was there that any sister ever asked me anything except my name or where I was from. It simply was not a part of the work; we did not need to exchange personal information to do the work.

I remember another story about an evangelical Protestant missionary who went to Mother for prayer. He wanted to know God's plan for his life. Mother immediately replied, "I will pray for you, but not for that. I will pray for faith, that is what you need—more faith." Mother Teresa said if God had told her his full plan for the Missionaries of Charity, she would have been too frightened to step out of the convent and pick up the first person on the street. She was simply called into a relationship with Christ that unfolded one day at a time.

The Missionaries' absolute conviction that they are serving Christ "in the distressing disguise of the poor" makes their arduous and repetitive labor sacred. Their confidence that God works through them grants them power, grace and humility. It is a very different task to bathe a soiled adult when you see him as Christ than if you are simply cleaning someone for your job. For them, each task must be done with love—small things done with great love.

At first their lives looked dreary to me—endless repetitions of tasks that I would relegate to a to-do list and then undertake with as much speed and efficiency as possible. They do nothing in this way; it is all done as if God himself is standing there. Noting the way volunteers would hurry in their work reaffirmed for Mother the necessity of the religious vocation. She said in an interview, "To persevere doing this work for a long time you need a greater power to push you from behind. Only religious life can give this power."[2]

The Mashis, too, understood this. One day while helping to do the wash, I remarked to a Mashi who spoke some English that with all these clothes and diapers every day, someone should donate a washer and dryer. I was quickly corrected by the woman who said gently, "Oh no, Jesus helps us wash. Love helps us." She reminded me of Brother Lawrence of the seventeenth century who accustomed himself to do everything for God and to be in his presence continually, so much so that he eventually found all things easy and pleasing, even the kitchen work to which he naturally had great aversion.[3]

Each morning, the Missionaries initiate this attitude of being in the presence of God through the Eucharist. Mother said, "We take Jesus from the altar to meet Jesus in the streets." For many Catholic Christians, much more than for Protestants, the sacrament of the Eucharist is a daily or weekly nourishment that they do not want to live without. Malcolm Muggeridge explained, "For Mother Teresa, faith is a personal relationship with God and the incarnate Christ; the Mass the spiritual food which sustains her."[4]

This understanding was critical to be a Missionary of Charity. Mother often told the story of a new Missionary from outside India who came to begin work in Calcutta. She was sent the first day to the Nirmal Hriday, the Home for the Dying, as is the custom. Mother told her as she left Mass, "You saw the priest during Holy Mass, with what love and care he touched Jesus in the bread. Do the same when you go to the Home, because it is the same Jesus you will find there in the broken bodies of our poor." And when the novice came back she had an enormous smile and said, "Mother, I have been touching the body of Christ for three hours." Mother asked what she did. The young woman exclaimed, "When we arrived there, they brought a man who had fallen into a drain, and been there for some time. He was covered with wounds and dirt and maggots, and I cleaned him and I knew I was touching the body of Christ!"[5]

This is a lesson for those of us in social services when we despair that our work may be changing nothing. Mother said in an interview,

> If we did not believe that this was the body of Christ, we would never be able to do this work. No amount of money could make us do it. It is He whom we reach in the people who are unwanted, unemployed, uncared for; they seem use-

less to society, nobody has time for them. It is just you and
I who must find them and help them. Often we pass them
without seeing them. But they are there for the finding.[6]

I began to think how differently I would work if I truly saw
each person I met as a hungry, hurting Christ. What if every time
someone came to me with a problem, I responded as though Christ
himself had approached me? What if I saw everyone all day long
as in need of a touch from God, and what if I were yielded enough
that God could actually use me to give his touch?

5

The Church as Flawed and Finite

>≤<

M ANY QUESTIONED MOTHER'S UNSWERVING allegiance to the
Catholic Church. She advised Muggeridge, who struggled with the
church, in a letter he later published, "The personal love Christ
has for you is infinite—the small difficulty you have regarding the
Church is finite. Overcome the finite with the infinite. Christ created you because he wanted you." She often said that what is hap-
pening on the surface of the church will pass, but Christ is the
same yesterday, today and tomorrow.[1] For her, the church was an
imperfect, finite vehicle through which she could express her love
and obedience to Christ, the infinite and perfect one, through acts
of love for the poor.

Like Muggeridge, I spent many years avoiding Christ because
Christians are not perfect. I could with great arrogance and equal
ignorance rail against the Crusades or the Inquisition (about
which I knew nothing), or some minister or priest in the news.
Finally I realized I could not continue to refuse God because the

people who call themselves by his name are imperfect, like me. Churches are imperfect in the same way and for the same reasons that businesses, schools, universities, families and nations are imperfect: they are filled with imperfect people.

Indeed if any of us could be perfect, God would not have sent his Son, Jesus, to take on flesh, live on earth and suffer death to forgive us our sins. With his power and grace we can continually transform, but in this life we will never be completely free of sin.

It would be gratifying, I suppose, if people could become good on their own. All utopian ideologies hold this to be true, as I once did. Invariably when I try to convince myself of my own goodness, my heart is lying. Pride creeps up when I think I do "right things." When I do "wrong things," I excuse them by comparing myself to others who may be worse, or I harden my heart to my sin and call it something else, usually by applying some currently popular psychological term. Pride used to keep me "surfing the spiritual net" for a spirituality that would confirm my deepest conviction that I was a good person.

C. S. Lewis wrote in *Mere Christianity* that Christians are not necessarily better than others, but everyone who becomes a Christian will be a better person than he or she would be without Christ.[2] This was freeing to me; it relieved me of arguments about the church or history. I finally realized that to avoid a relationship with God because of the Crusades or because I disagree with my neighbor's behavior is simply irrational. By the daily grace of God, I see more clearly my own arrogance, self-righteousness and sinfulness, yet I know I was far worse in all ways before. Moreover, I know when I criticize leaders or institutions, it is just the evil in my own heart being played out on a larger scale.[3]

How unbearable is the knowledge of myself without Christ's forgiveness and promise to free me from my brokenness! I could not even approach true self-knowledge before I followed

Christ; the truth was too painful without a remedy. It astounds and saddens me that so few choose the salvation which is so simple and pure and available to everyone—rich or poor, brilliant or simple, young or old.[4] Of course I should not be surprised; my pride kept me away. Like Paul, I can always say,

> So I find it to be a law that when I want to do right, evil lies close at hand. For I delight in the law of God, in my inner being, but I see in my members another law waging war against the law of my mind and making me captive to the law of sin that dwells in my members. Wretched man that I am! Who will deliver me from this body of death? Thanks be to God through Jesus Christ our Lord![5]

Mother simply said, "I can do nothing good on my own, I am totally dependent on God."

6

Do All Things Without
Complaining or Disputing

⫷⫸

ABOUT A MONTH INTO MY WORK in Calcutta, three European women arrived to volunteer. They were health care professionals and were also assigned to Shishu Bhavan. Despite Mother Teresa's persistent admonitions that the sisters did not run hospitals, these women must have expected Shishu to look like a pediatrics ward. One of the sisters at Shishu was a trained nurse, and children who were taken to the hospital received medicines and instructions. Sometimes doctors volunteered their time to visit each bedside with the sisters. The sister in charge kept a meticulous, handwritten record for every child in an old, yellowed notebook—medicines administered at what time, the child's temperature, etc. That is where the similarities with a hospital ended.

These women spotted a young girl who was congested and, incidentally, already on medication. They asked where they might find the respiratory therapy machine. However, the Missionaries own very little equipment of any kind. When these volunteers heard this, they became angry and began to argue with the sister in charge, who happened to be the trained nurse. Surely, they protested, Mother Teresa had the money to buy a respiratory therapy machine. The sister stood politely, hands clasped at her chest and respectfully nodded to indicate she was listening.

Getting little response from the Missionaries, the women turned to riling up other volunteers with whom they found more sympathy. One complaint led to another. It reminded me of many teachers' lounges, offices and faculty meetings. How easily one derogatory comment leads to another, and soon the spirit of the place is rife with anger, frustration and discouragement. Even humor is often a cruel verbal assault on others. I stopped going on breaks at this time as I found it decreased my energy for the rest of the day's work. I know teachers who have stopped frequenting the teachers' lounge for similar reasons.

The effect of the volunteers' anger was not limited to the adults. Many of the children's handicaps made it difficult for them to eat. As I watched these women feeding the children, I noticed that the children were having even more difficulty than usual eating. Some refused the food, others cried. The women were not angry with the children, but the spirit of anger spilled over into everything they did.

One of the most difficult things about learning to live in Christ is overcoming the tendency to live by feelings and over-rationalized imaginations. Perhaps it is an occupational hazard, but I often think that just because I know a truth in my mind, I am acting on it. But knowledge alone is no guarantee of actions. This is the reason why so many campaigns to educate people about the adverse effects of drugs, cigarettes and alcohol fail; and why successful programs like Alcoholics Anonymous begin by acknowledging human weakness and divine power. It is not that we do not know in our

minds what is right or best; it is that our minds alone are too weak
to control our will, and our spirits too underdeveloped to control
either. Our spirits are made to be filled with God's Spirit and thus
have primacy over our body, mind, will and emotions.[1]

In this instance, the women's toxic emotions over the lack of a
respiratory machine infected the entire room. Convinced of the
need for such a machine, the volunteers arrived later in the week
with a portable respiratory therapy machine which they had bor-
rowed or rented from somewhere. The sisters gratefully agreed
for them to use it. Yet still the women's attitudes did not change
much; they found many more things to criticize throughout the
couple of weeks they volunteered. Though I am certain they de-
sired to help and were not aware of the effects, they left a damag-
ing spirit of anger in their wake.

The Missionaries seemed aware of the danger. They did not get
involved and said nothing. Regarding the whole incident, I only
heard one remark from a sister. I commented while feeding the
infants that the European women must have gone home. Sister
Delphinus said gently, "Isn't it wonderful how God sent those
volunteers with that machine at just the right moment for that
child!" She had not let herself become embittered by the wom-
en's attitudes. She was describing one of God's miracles while the
bearers of the miracle had not even noticed. The Missionaries'
spiritual eyes are always open to instances of divine providence;
luck or coincidence have no place in their worldview. Unlike me,
their godly spirits largely drive their actions.

Hearing the Missionary's comment, I thought to myself that no
matter how long a discussion were to be extended between these
women and the sisters, their conversations would never meet.
Their assumptions about the world were too different. No wonder
the Missionaries rarely spoke with us; we hardly would have understood them.

The Missionaries could afford no compromises with harmful spirits. They fervently clung to the worldview of Christ and resisted polluting it by arguing with people who perhaps could not really understand it. A unity of worldview must be an enormous advantage of living within a religious community. Yet they treated each of us guests as though we too were Christ. They modeled the admonition from Paul, "Do all things without grumbling or questioning, that you may be blameless and innocent, children of God without blemish in the midst of a crooked and twisted generation, among whom you shine as lights in the world."[2]

Mother taught that

> criticism is nothing less than dressed up pride. It eats up all the love of God. A truly generous soul must never stoop to criticism. As a rule, people who criticize never do it openly, but go about doing it in a whisper. Refrain from prejudice, which means to set your mind against somebody. It is very sad when it becomes a part of our lives.[3]

I had originally thought that part of the peace I felt around the Missionaries was their strong tendency to introversion and prayer. I was to learn very late in my trip that the other reason they did not speak much with us is that they have a rule that no one is to speak during the day's work unless it is necessary to get the work done; rather, they are to pray unceasingly.[4] I thought how different most workplaces, my own included, would be with this simple rule. Even though I know the effect of my various emotions on others and on my work, how hard it is to work simply in the spirit of Christ.

7

It All Belongs to God

Every morning at nine, the side gate to the patio at Shishu Bhavan was opened and the sisters served food to anyone who came from the streets. A couple of times the babies were quiet enough that I could walk down and watch. The sisters had plates, utensils and an enormous vat of warm food, usually a mixture of rice, dal and vegetables. Since most people in India are Hindu and vegetarian—and meat in Calcutta is expensive and chancy due to the lack of refrigeration—the protein-rich rice and dal is a mainstay of most meals. The Missionaries also have no refrigeration; they buy their food daily from the markets, just like the poor. The Missionaries ate the same food.

First the sisters fed the hungry people who came without even a plate. These were the poorest of the poorest, and they could have as much as they liked. They were most often the elderly or the disabled, abandoned by their families, incapable of work and living on the streets. Next in line stood women with pots of various sizes to take food to their families. The vat of food never seemed to run out. It mattered not if the same people came every day or only once in their lifetime.

Someone once asked Mother if she was spoiling the poor, to which she replied, "There are many congregations who spoil the rich, it is good to have one congregation in the name of the poor to spoil the poor." Father Angelo Scolozzi, who worked with Mother for over twenty years, remembers that when she said this, the room fell silent for a long while.[1]

One week, a rumor circulated that a few of the women who had filled their pots in the morning were selling the food on the street. The volunteers who saw it confronted the Missionary in charge. She simply and calmly replied, "Not to worry. It all belongs to God." She was not going to spend any energy or time policing the food or scrutinizing the people who came for help. If there were a problem, God would have to take care of it. After all, it was his food and work. The rumor soon lost its force.

The Missionaries of Charity do not concern themselves with controlling what they have; they simply give it away. There are no criteria or qualification procedures for receiving help from the Missionaries. If you come one day or every day, it does not matter to them. They do not fret about things that might make them less effective in their mission to serve the poorest of the poor. If they hear of families who are ill or hungry, two sisters go to them with food. If the family cannot cook, they cook it for them. If the family has no strength, they feed them, clean up afterward and return until the family can manage again on their own. They do not analyze the worthiness of people or the cause of their poverty; they simply act as quickly as possible to the best of their ability.

To the Missionaries, poverty is first a spiritual problem and only secondarily a political one. Mother Teresa said, "I won't mix in politics. War is the fruit of politics, and so I don't involve myself, that's all. If I get stuck in politics, I will stop loving. Because I will have to stand by one, not by all. This is the difference."[2]

Subsequently, no bureaucracy or political talk characterized the Missionaries' homes. I read once that in highly bureaucratized cultures, people stop asking, is this right or good? They substitute the question, is it legal, or can I get away with it? The Missionaries' ethos of prompt and personal care left little time to debate. They saw a need and filled it with God's provisions. Neither were they obsessed with perfection; they were devoted to being faithful to the little things.

Probably one of the most profound statements in the Bible for living in our times is found in the Psalms: "Fret not yourself; it tends only to evil."[3] I see so many instances in my own life when I waste time fretting over a task that I could do in a fraction of the time were I in the right spirit. I sometimes fritter away hours figuring out what can be done, what it will take to continue, what may go wrong or, worse, asking myself if I really want to do it. All this lessens the quality, quantity and timeliness of my work. The Missionaries, instead, prayerfully commit their worries to God and act without stopping to question.

8

There Is Always Enough

MOTHER TERESA AND THE MISSIONARIES of Charity never ask for money. They do no fundraising and allow no one to do it for them. It is against the rules of their Constitution. Mother said,

> We do not accept anything, neither church maintenance, nor salary, nor anything for the work we do, all over the world. Every Missionary of Charity is the poorest of the poor. That is why we can do anything. Whatever is given to the poor is the same for us. We wear the kind of clothes they wear. But ours is a choice. We choose that way. To be able to understand the poor, we must know what is poverty. Otherwise we will speak a different language, no? We won't be able to come close to that mother who is anxious for her child. We depend on providence. We are like the trees, like the flowers. But we are more important to Him than the flowers or the grass. He takes care of them; He takes much greater care of us.[1]

They are completely dependent on God for all the resources to carry out his work. Mother Teresa believed that as long as they were faithful to what God called them to, it was his job to provide—divine providence. In cases when food and resources are not available, they may beg for food to give to the poor. This evidently happened upon occasion in the early years. She herself left the convent to serve the poorest of the poor with less than a dollar in her pocket.

When I was there, the Missionaries fasted the first Friday of every month and set aside the money they would have otherwise spent on their own food. It went into an emergency fund for special needs of the poor. I met a young woman who had grown up with the Missionaries since childhood, and they were sending her to explore colleges with part of the fund. The Missionaries sometimes help widows pay for their children's education.

There were few toys or books at the centers. I learned from the Mashis, sisters, volunteers and children just how much can be done with a scrap of paper and crayon, or by telling stories with hands and singing. The lack of toys concerned no one except an occasional volunteer, like me. I realized more clearly how Americans are accustomed to having so many things that we have trouble coping without them. In the United States, we are entertained day and night; we can hardly live our own lives for living others' lives—fictional or real—through movies, television and the news. Both children and adults who have many things constantly want more, and then in a short while, we are restless and bored again. I often feel the compulsive lure of the material. Every so often, I "simplify" by getting rid of my unused things. But a year later, I need to do it all over again. To my shame my garage is bursting with boxes, the contents of which I no longer even remember. By contrast, the Missionaries and children live in the present; they entertain one another with whatever simple objects lay at hand or without them.

I thought much about how schools, universities, hospitals and businesses all believe they need money to implement change. No doubt money sometimes helps, but I became convinced as I worked with the Missionaries that the changes institutions need most are not material ones. Rather, they need changes of heart in those of us who work in them—imperfect people working with other imperfect people to the best of our ability with great attitudes. This is so much more possible with God's grace than on our own.

Because of Mother Teresa's belief in divine providence and because she never solicited money, she had no need to check the references of her donors. Mother's money came from those on the left and the right, the rich and the poor. She said, "I have never been in need but I accept whatever people give me for the poor. I never refuse them because they have a right to give in charity. I accept whatever."[2] However, her strongest critic, Christopher Hitchens, accused her of taking money from people who had made their fortunes through questionable dealings, oppressive political regimes, or simply the "politically incorrect." Hitchens's book had just come out while I was in Calcutta and I read it there.[3] One of the donors specifically mentioned in it was Charles Keating of the savings and loan scandal in California.

At that time, I also happened to be reading the Hebrew Proverbs and found three verses that explained perfectly how she was the recipient of these monies. First, while it is written that "wealth gained hastily will dwindle," another verse is even more specific: "he who increases his wealth by exorbitant interest amasses it for another who will be kind to the poor."[4] This explains the vulnerability of those who had invested in the scheme. A third verse states that "a sinner's wealth is laid up for the righteous." This explains how the transfer happened from those who were responsible for promoting the scheme to the Missionaries of Charity.[5] As

I read the Bible in the afternoons, I was learning that this book hides incredible wisdom about all aspects of life—psychology, sociology, economics, business and philosophy.

Perhaps, as Hitchens implies, she did receive quite a bit of money once she became famous. I certainly hope so. But Mother Teresa had been picking up the poor and destitute since 1948, long before she ever became a household name. Father Angelo, who worked closely with her for twenty years, told me that eventually she asked the Vatican to set up a bank account for them. To the Missionaries who never ask for money, it is God's business how and how much is given them. They simply trust their needs will be met and receive the gifts with grateful hearts.

For Mother Teresa the only problem money posed was if it stood in the way of their mission. If money from the church, government or an individual came with strings attached that began to dictate their work, then and only then would it have to be refused. For example, they almost did not open a center in Phoenix because the city council initially insisted on air conditioning. They stripped the lush accommodations in a home in San Francisco to match their simple and poor lifestyle.

Hitchens also accused Mother of receiving the best in health care when it was not available to the poor. However, I took an offer to her from a colleague's brother, who was involved in developing a new pacemaker, to replace her old pacemaker with the new and much improved one. She said she could not accept it, but she would accept it for the poor. She refused another medical offer of a world-renowned acupressurist. When I called and repeated these offers upon her becoming more ill a few months after I left, she again refused and asked for prayers instead. My impression is that she mostly received good health care when she was too ill to fight it. Some of her poor did receive quality health care since, from the beginning of her work, she was a genius at inspiring doctors to provide free service to the poor.

I began to realize that the principle of divine providence is one that defies all principles of economics that underlie our current philosophies and theories. From capitalism to communism, economic theories all assume a scarcity of resources. Divine providence assumes that God has provided an abundance for every need.

Divine providence is not merely about money, it is an attitude toward life of trust in God. Jean De Caussade, eighteenth-century author of *Abandonment to Divine Providence,* wrote that

> when God lives in us, we have nothing to help us beyond what he gives us moment by moment. Nothing else is provided and no road is marked out. . . . Our only satisfaction must be to live in the present moment as if there were nothing to expect beyond it. If what happens to a soul abandoned to God is all that is necessary for it, it is clear that it can lack nothing and that it should never complain, for this would show that it lacked faith and was living by the light of its reason and the evidence of its senses.[6]

I realized this principle was one of the reasons I had prayed that the Missionaries would only say yes to my coming if it was God's will. The reason they said yes and the reason my trip came together effortlessly was that it was his will.

Radical faith in divine providence is why Mother Teresa could tell her sisters one night when there was no bread for the next day, "Earnestly pray and go to bed; tomorrow, if need be, we will beg on the streets to feed the poor." And why the next morning some schools in the area closed unexpectedly, and a truckload of bread destined for the schools was delivered to the Missionaries.[7]

9

The Vow of Poverty and
Service to the Poor

THE MISSIONARIES OF CHARITY commit themselves to four vows: poverty, chastity, obedience and free service to the poorest of the poor. Mother believed that these vows formed the pillars upon which their lives could flourish in Christ. If any one were to be removed, everything would collapse. These vows keep the Missionaries free to follow Christ, free from evil and able to make reparation for the sins of excess in the world such as materialism, greed, lust, disobedience and rebellion.

The Missionaries of Charity live in the neighborhoods of the poorest of the poor and live like them. They wash their clothes in a pail and on the concrete; in Calcutta they live without refrigeration, heating, air conditioning or even hot water. Every Missionary has three saris—one is washed while the other is worn, and a third is kept for special occasions such as holy days. Their only personal possessions include a bucket for washing, a bowl, a cup, glass, cutlery, two sheets, a pillow and pillowcase, a rope belt, a pair of sandals, a crucifix pin that holds part of the sari together, a rosary, a Bible, as well as a printed prayer book and songbooks, which have been typed on manual typewriters and covered with brown paper bags. They can pack all their belongings into a small box and be ready to move to another part of the world at a moment's notice. They sleep on cots in large rooms together. They sit and kneel on concrete floors in the chapels.[1] They travel by foot or use the least expensive mode of transportation.[2]

As a result of this, the Missionaries understand the special demands that poverty makes. It was almost inconceivable to me the time it took to accomplish even the smallest task without the conveniences to which I am accustomed in the West. I heard an African pastor once say that 60 percent of the world sleeps on the floor or ground and eats with their hands, which is not difficult to believe when you are in India.[3] The Missionaries truly live the life of those they serve to the greatest extent possible.

When I was there, the Mashis, volunteers and children ate cookies that had been donated at Christmas by a large company in Germany. The Missionaries never ate them. Sister Delphinus told me with great joy that the Missionaries celebrate the day after Christmas and the day after Easter with a bowl of ice cream served by Mother. One day a young girl kept insisting that Sister Delphinus take and eat some snack mix. She struggled to resist; the child dropped it in her lap and Sister promptly tucked it in my hand as soon as the girl was not looking. Her urgent expression made me know to take it. Afterward we gave it to some of the other children.

One result of their firsthand knowledge of poverty is that they do not treat poor parents as the enemies of poor children. They value and seek to serve the whole family. I thought of how some of the excellent teachers I know in urban American schools have chosen to live in the poor neighborhoods where they teach. Others attend events in the neighborhood with their students, or take students to other parts of the city on weekends and holidays. They make every effort to develop relationships with the students' parents. They know no matter how tough life gets, most of these parents care very deeply for their children and their children for them.

As the Missionaries walk through the streets to work or shop for food, they come to know the families well. They learn daily of any needs—families with no food, children whose mother is too ill to care for them, or a person passed out on the streets. They may serve an ill parent with food and medicine while keeping their children at the center. Once informed of a crisis, the Missionaries head out two-by-two or four-by-four to help. A Missionary of Charity never goes alone.

When I first arrived, I thought they lived like the poor solely to understand them better. While this obviously happens, it is not the only reason they have chosen such serious vows of poverty and free service to the poorest of the poor. They embrace their poverty for four reasons that I could discern. First, Mother Teresa always spoke of how God had chosen to visit the earth as a poor man—Jesus, born in a stable, owning only the clothes on his back, having no dwelling place of his own. Second, she wrote and spoke about how being poor afforded protection from evil, for they could not be easily tempted to do things for the wrong reasons or indulge their own appetites. Third, she believed they could understand and serve the poor better if they were poor. Last, Mother believed that their voluntary poverty made some reparation for the material sins of the world, for the abuse of wealth.

Nevertheless, Mother Teresa did not believe that God calls everyone to live in poverty or to work in the same way with the poor. In fact, she said that some were called to live in castles. That is why she could just as easily minister to Princess Diana as to the poorest of the poor. She told a group of volunteers, "It is not a sin to be rich," but be careful because "riches can suffocate you if they are not used in the right way."[4]

Mother told me how people in the West are poor. In fact, she considered us the poorest of the poor spiritually because our physical comfort makes us believe we do not need God and our busyness makes us ignore him. Sociologists tell us that the poor are not necessarily more likely to be religious, but they tend to be more fervent in their beliefs than the middle class and wealthy.[5] In addition, the wealthiest nations in the West are now considered "post-Christian."[6] In fact, Mother sent sisters and brothers to the United States because she sensed we were in spiritual trouble. That is how I met Father Angelo; he had come to work with oyster farmers in south Texas at the request of Mother.

The Missionaries are called to live among and serve not just the poor but the "poorest of the poor." In Mother's mind, the Missionaries owed the poor a great deal for helping them to love God better. She said in an interview,

> I believe the people of today do not think that the poor are like them as human beings. They look down on them. But if they had that deep respect for the dignity of the poor people, I am sure it would be easy for them to come closer to them and to see that they too are children of God, and they have as much right to the things of life and of love and of service as anybody else.[7]

The Constitution of the Missionaries of Charity defines the poorest of the poor:

> We give immediate and effective service to the poorest of the poor, as long as they have no one to help them, by
>
> - feeding the hungry: not only with food but also with the Word of God;

- giving drink to the thirsty: not only for water, but for knowledge, peace, truth, justice, and love;
- clothing the naked: not only with clothes, but also with human dignity;
- giving shelter to the homeless: not only a shelter made of bricks but a heart that understands, that covers, that loves;
- nursing the sick and dying: not only the body, but also the mind and spirit.

The poorest of the poor, materially and spiritually, irrespective of caste, creed or nationality are: the hungry; the thirsty; the naked; the homeless; the ignorant; the captives; the crippled; the leprosy sufferers; the alcoholics; the sick and dying destitutes; the unloved; the abandoned; the outcast; all those who are a burden to human society, who have lost all hope and faith in life; all hard-hearted persistent sinners; those under the power of the evil one; those who are leading others to sin, error or confusion; the atheists; the erring; those in confusion and doubt; the tempted; the spiritually blind, weak, lax and ignorant; those not yet touched by the light of Christ; the hungry for the Word and peace of God; the difficult; the repulsive; the sorrowful; the souls in purgatory; and every Missionary of Charity by accepting to live the life of evangelical poverty and by the very fact of being sinners.

I found it interesting that Mother considered hard-hearted sinners and atheists among the poorest of the poor. Surely this had been true of me. The Constitution continues:

In fulfillment of our special mission in the church following the lowliness of Christ, we remain right on the ground by living Christ's concern for the poorest and the lowliest and by being of immediate but effective service to them until they find some others who can help in a better and more lasting way.[8]

"Right on the ground" is exactly where they serve. Radical feminist Germaine Greer criticized Mother, calling her "the glamour-girl of poverty."[9] One of her criticisms was that the Missionaries did nothing to cure poverty in the world. Rather they just helped a few people.

To these types of criticisms Mother once responded, "You take care of their tomorrows; I take care of their todays."[10] Upon my return, I had an exchange with a rabbi who told me how much more he appreciated twentieth-century contemplative monk Thomas Merton's writings on poverty than Mother Teresa's approach. Being an academic, I knew what he admired in Merton's intellectual prose and poetry, but I wondered how much Merton's work really resulted in feeding the poorest of the poor. Similarly, did my research and teaching about the education of the poor ever really help the poor?

10

The Vow of Obedience

Obedience has become almost a dirty word in our culture. To the Missionaries it is a vow. They are to obey the sister in charge as Mother obeyed the ecclesiastical authorities—no matter what. Unless one is asked to disobey God's law, obedience to and prayer for those in authority is the rule. In this obedience, the sister is conforming to God's order. Mother Teresa wrote:

> Jesus, the only Begotten Son of the Father, equal to his Father, God from God, Light from Light, did not feel it below his dignity to obey. Therefore, we will:
> accept, love and respect all our lawful superiors
> sincerely pray for them
> show joyful trust in and loyalty to them
> make our obedience cheerful, prompt, simple, and
>   constant without question or excuse.
> We should obey the known wish of our superiors as well as their commands in a spirit of faith.[1]

After Mother's call within a call to leave the Sisters of Loreto to serve the poorest, she said, "I knew where I belonged, but I did not know how to get there. . . . I had the blessing of obedience."[2] She carefully checked her call with all her authorities. She believed when she lay before them what Jesus had said to her, they would also hear from God, and their leading and counsel would assure her that the call was real. She did not want to start an order if God did not ordain it. Her obedience, even in the face of what seemed great delays (four years), was her guarantee that God was directing and would continue to bless her.

As with all obedience to authority, it becomes even more critical that those who lead strive to increase in godliness. The Constitution also embodies this:

> The superior of each house, however, will remember that she is first for the sisters and next for the work. Therefore, let all her dealings with the sisters be motherly, never discouraging them, especially in failure; she encourages and joyfully welcomes each member to make a personal and valuable contribution to the well-being of the Society and the Church. . . . She will take proper care of the old and the sick and of those who do not look after themselves; in the house work she will always be the first to devote herself; she will have nothing special or different in food, clothes, or lodging; she will trust her sisters completely and be generous always when the sisters observe poverty well.[3]

She wanted the houses to be houses of love, joy and peace.[4]

I grew up in a culture hit hard by the 1960s when universities broke out in various anti-authority movements from free love, to anti-war, to radical feminism. Obedience, to me, indicated anything from a lack of intelligence, to absence of creativity, to giving into a system presumed unjust, evil, or at best, inadequate. "I did it my way," the song title exclaims. To be different and defiant were badges of honor. I remember my own intoxication with these movements beginning in the early 1970s. Even popular media, music, television and movies often project disobedience as a kind of valor, a form of humor, a sign of intelligence, cleverness or superiority. All these continue to support a culture of disobedience, the spirit of rebellion. Even the social sciences and humanities are still often better at criticizing those in authority—individuals, laws, ideas, strategies—than at fostering new ways to solve problems.

Mother believed that criticism weakens our will to obey and that our will is the only thing that God will not take from us. Mother Teresa wrote to her sisters, "It is much easier to conquer a country than to conquer ourselves. Every act of disobedience weakens my spiritual life. It is like a wound letting out every drop of one's blood. Nothing can cause this havoc in our spiritual life as quickly as disobedience."[5]

I wondered how much damage had been done to my spiritual life for having joined, enjoyed and taught rebelliousness. I remembered the fear and exhilaration of attending protests of all kinds and the self-satisfied arrogance of arguing against almost every political act, generally with great ignorance, as well. My rebelliousness did not change things for the better. My rebelliousness set my will free of boundaries, and in so doing I was actually less free and more dependent on being like everyone else around me. My rebellion had taken me a long way in the wrong direction. Now I was called to be a servant of Christ. As twentieth-century philosopher Simone Weil said, "We have to make ourselves slaves and beggars to follow Christ."[6]

II

The Vow of Chastity

>≈<

IF OBEDIENCE IS OUT OF FASHION, certainly chastity, the third vow of the Missionaries, is the only other virtue even more countercultural. The Missionaries pledge all their affections to Christ. This is what makes their poverty and obedience more possible, because their desires are focused entirely on Jesus. Mother and the Missionaries celebrate chastity as an essential part of their total surrender to God. She wrote:

> The vow of chastity liberates us totally for the contemplation of God and the wholehearted and free service of the poorest of the poor. By it we cleave to Jesus with an undivided love so as to:
>
> - live in him, for him, by him and with him as our sole guide,
> - be invaded by his own holiness and filled with his own Spirit of love,

- show forth the luminous face of Jesus, radiant with purity and love for the Father and mankind,

- make reparation to God for all the sins of the flesh committed in the world today.[1]

She said of the struggle to be chaste:

> In my heart there is only one vacant seat. It is for God and nobody else. Temptation is like fire in which gold is purified. So we have to go through this fire. The temptations are allowed by God. The only thing we have to do is to refuse to give in. If I say I do not want it, I am safe. There may be temptations against purity, against faith, against my vocation. If we love our vocation, we will be tempted. But then we will also grow in sanctity. We have to fight temptation for the love of God.
>
> The vow of chastity does not diminish us; it makes us live to the full if it is kept properly. The vow of chastity is not simply a list of don'ts—it is love. I give myself to God and I receive God. God becomes my own because I become his own. That is why I become completely dedicated to him by the vow of chastity. God does not want to impose a burden on us by the vow of chastity. We must love our consecration, which sets us apart for God alone.[2]

Chilean theologian Jorge Cardinal Medina Estévez, in his lovely book on marriage and the family, notes that there are two forms of chastity, "one that is proper to the unmarried—single or widowed persons—and another that corresponds to those who are married."[3] Estévez writes that marriage "is a very important expression of love and the means of fruitfulness chosen by God. Here this union is 'a true union,' that is to say, it is a sign of the union of Christ with his Church, expressing a mutual self-giving that is faithful and loving and sealed by the sacrament until death."[1] The reason Christians are to remain pure before marriage is that "a love that is pure means that when the time comes to marry, the consent will be freer, motivated solely by love. When love has not been pure, bonds of dependence arise that create feelings of obligation, something that is not healthy or advantageous for the couple."[5]

Of celibate chastity, the kind the Missionaries embrace, Estévez says it is voluntary, done for the sake of the kingdom of heaven, and a gift. It does not involve contempt for sexuality, a selfish avoidance of responsibility or disdain for marriage. "Rather it is a call from God, of a 'vocation.'"[6] This calling of celibacy is described by Paul in his first letter to the Corinthians:

> I want you to be free from anxieties. The unmarried man is anxious about the things of the Lord, how to please the Lord. But the married man is anxious about worldly things, how to please his wife, and his interests are divided. And the unmarried or betrothed woman is anxious about the things of the Lord, how to be holy in body and spirit. But the married woman is anxious about worldly things, how to please her husband. I say this for your own benefit, not to lay any restraint upon you, but to promote good order and to secure your undivided devotion to the Lord.
>
> If anyone thinks that he is not behaving properly toward his betrothed, if his passions are strong, and it has to be, let him do as he wishes: let them marry—it is no sin. But whoever is firmly established in his heart, being under no necessity but having his desire under control, and has determined this in his heart, to keep her as his betrothed, he will do well.[7]

Certainly most people are not called to a lifetime of chastity, but for a time, many young people are—just as I was. Before knowing

God, we women have known men, and our way back to God is made more difficult. Our whole identities often are wrapped up in what men think of us before we even know our own selves and, more critically, before we know who we are in God. To Mother Teresa, beauty was in the heart that belonged to God.

I had been "serially monogamous," and I was perfectly at home in the culture in which I lived; I was normal, maybe even better, because I was faithful in my relationships—until the next one. I had grown up with soap operas, movies and television, which depicted my behavior as exciting and fairly normal. I had gone from that to the more erotic films and even pornography.[8] My first forty-one years had left God with a giant task of cleaning up.

By the time I was at Mother Teresa's, I had been chaste for three years, but the struggle had been a long and difficult one. I had to confess thoughts that would frequently intrude involuntarily and totally depend on the faithfulness and grace of God. I clung to the Scripture that promises, "If we confess our sins, he is faithful and just to forgive us our sins and to cleanse us from all unrighteousness."[9] After three years, God had cleansed my mind tremendously.

Mother said of their call to lifelong celibacy, "God is purity himself; nothing impure can come before him. . . . God loves us in spite of our misery and sinfulness. He is our loving Father and so we have only to turn to him. . . . But impurity is an obstacle to seeing God. This doesn't mean only the sin of impurity, but any attachment, anything that takes us away from God, anything that makes us less Christlike, any hatred, any uncharitableness is also impurity. If we are full of sin, God cannot fill what is full. That is why we need forgiveness to become empty, and then God fills us with himself."[10] She said, "It is the vow of chastity that gives us the freedom to love everybody. We must be free of things to be full of God."[11]

Small Things with Great Love

MOTHER TERESA WAS BORN Agnes Gonxha in 1910 in Albania, but when she became a nun, she took the name "Teresa."
This was after Therese of Lisieux, a young nun in France in the
late 1800s who had coined the phrase "small things with great
love." I had my own instruction on "small things with great love"
while in Calcutta.

The first day I noticed a very tiny infant, Babloo. I learned that
he was born prematurely and at three months still only weighed
seven pounds. Shortly after his birth, he had contracted an intestinal virus against which medicine was of no avail. The sisters kept
him alive as best they could and prayed that his body would be
able to overcome the virus. He had lived most of his life at Shishu.
His Muslim parents were very poor and feared they would not be
able to save him. His mother came once a week to visit, feed and
hold him. A French woman described him aptly one day when
she said, "He looks like a baby bird that has fallen from his nest."

He was the tiniest of the infants, yet his wrinkled skin made him look like an old man.

Because he looked so fragile, other volunteers shied away from him. And because he did not cry much, he was often alone. I began regularly feeding him and massaging his muscles with oil as the French woman had taught me. I tried to get him to make eye contact, which he did relatively easily. Soon I loved this infant in a way that is hard to describe.

I soon realized that while all the other young infants were drinking four to eight ounces at every feeding in a relatively short period, Babloo could only finish about an ounce or two in the same amount of time and then be off to sleep. I spoke to Sister Delphinus about my observation and she said, "Let's pray." She taught me her favorite prayer she had memorized in childhood, and we said it together. Then she said confidently that God would help us. The prayer was the Anima Christi that we said each morning after Mass:

> Soul of Christ, sanctify me
> Body of Christ, save me
> Blood of Christ, inebriate me
> Water from Christ's side, wash me
> Passion of Christ, strengthen me
> O good Jesus, hear me
> Within Thy wounds hide me
> Suffer me not to be separated from Thee
> From the malicious enemy defend me
> In the hour of my death call me
> And bid me come unto Thee
> That I may praise Thee with Thy saints
> and with Thy angels
> Forever and ever
> Amen[1]

Naively, I wasn't sure this prayer would work; I wondered why we did not just pray specifically for Babloo. So much for my doubts. The next day, a woman came in donating glass bottles with various nipples. I noted that one nipple was much smaller than the others. We tried it, and Babloo found it much easier to drink from. I also noticed, through my own clumsiness one day, that when I left the bottle cap slightly loose, it was even easier for him to drink. So after that we used a diaper to catch the drip. We began to notice his every move and tried many things—playing patty cake, singing and all manner of cajoling—to get him to stay awake for more food. He seemed to like songs with the word *alleluia*. I sang to him softly and in a far corner because I cannot really carry a tune. Now that I think about it, perhaps that is what really kept him awake for more formula! He particularly liked the hymn "Seek Ye First," which is one of my favorites as well. However, one day, one of the older and sterner sisters approached me and questioned my choice of songs. It was Lent; "alleluia" is not sung in the Catholic church during Lent. I told her Babloo liked songs with the "A-word." Without a smile, she promptly informed me that God would forgive me.

One thing led to another and soon the sister and I had Babloo drinking four ounces in a single sitting. However, the first few days it took about two hours to feed him four ounces. Gradually his strength and capacity increased until he could drink the four ounces like any of our other hungry fellows. He began to grow steadily.

I learned a great deal from this small infant. First, it takes much more time and concentration to do small things with love. Who would have thought it could take two hours to feed a child as tiny as he? Actually many of the children there needed great love and patience at feeding time. Mother Teresa used to say, "There is nothing small to God, once you give it to God, it is infinite."

Brother Lawrence, a seventeenth-century monk, exhorted:

We ought not to be weary of doing little things for the love of
God, who regards not the greatness of the work, but the love
with which it is performed. We should not wonder if, in the
beginning, we often fail in our endeavors, but that at last we
shall gain a habit, which will naturally produce its acts in us,
without our care, and to our exceeding great delight.[2]

One night while holding Babloo's tiny body, I realized that he
and I were like ships passing and exchanging encouragement to
one another. To live, he needed to attach himself to the world; for
me to live, I needed to detach myself from it. I needed to live more
in the spirit where he seemed to be suspended in uncertainty.

13

Prayer Is Our First Work

≽⊰

I COMMENTED ONE DAY TO ONE OF the sisters who was scurrying from one task to the next at how hard she worked. She looked at me as though she had not ever thought of it that way. Then she said, "Oh, but our first work is prayer."

When most of us look at the Missionaries of Charity, we see their physical labor—cooking, scrubbing, feeding, cleaning, tending the poor, picking people up off the streets or visiting shut-ins. But few know that Mother Teresa and the Missionaries see their first work as prayer and the work with the poor as a natural outcome of that prayer. They intentionally stop to pray six times a day in addition to praying as they go to and from their destinations and work. Mother wrote that these are times during the day "when we can regain our strength and fill up our emptiness with Jesus."[1]

Mother Teresa called the Missionaries "contemplatives at the heart of the world." They are contemplative because prayer is their life. It binds them to God, reveals to them his will, and secures his blessing and protection all day long. Yet they also live and work in the heart of the world—in slums and in the midst of the most pressing needs.

A group of people who suffer from chronic pain and disease have formed the Sick and Suffering Co-Workers of the Missionaries of Charity. These people offer up their sufferings and prayers for a particular Missionary every day, and that same Missionary prays each day for the coworker.

Mother fell during my visit and broke her collarbone. After her two-day stay in the hospital, she was back at Mass. She looked tired and worn. I will never forget how she grabbed onto my arm her first day back and looked at me and said, "Please pray for me." I wanted to cry. Was it not I who needed her to pray for me? I felt unworthy of the task, but God convicted me of my initial reluctance. I felt I did not know how to pray, but I began in earnest to pray on my way there and back, as the Missionaries do in their travels. I carried a small, wooden prayer ring with ten beads in my pocket and prayed for Mother, the sisters, friends and family, and for Calcutta. At each wooden bead I would send up a prayer and then on to the next one. The first three years after my conversion, I slept with a small wooden cross on a metal keychain wrapped around one of my fingers so that when I awoke at night I would remember God. The wooden prayer ring became my daytime reminder to pray.

One day Babloo became extremely ill. When I entered the room that morning, I saw him wrapped in a blanket. In the heat of Calcutta, there had to be something very wrong. I rushed to his bassinet, fearing he had died, but he was hanging on. Soon the Missionary in charge was trying to thread an IV into an arm not much thicker than two fingers. With special permission, I stayed all day, trying to comfort and feed him as an IV slowly dripped into his veins. Some of the older children stopped by his bedside that day.

Exploring the IV, they became vigilant, even prayerful, around his crib. I had seen them do this around the beds of some young boys who had been burned.

About six in the evening, I thought I would go down to the Mother House for Adoration and pray for him. However, about that time he began to wake up and wanted to play. I felt the Lord saying, "Adore me through him." It was the first time I came close to understanding the way the Missionaries understood their work. I stayed and began to really contemplate what it had taken for this tiny infant to have clung to life for four long months despite the virus that racked his frame.

By seven o'clock, he and I were both almost asleep. One of the sisters gently touched my shoulder and asked if I would like to join them in their own chapel for Adoration because we would pray for Babloo. She said the superior of the house had said it was okay if I joined them. I was delighted because we were not generally allowed to worship at the sites where we worked, only at the Mother House. We prayed that night, and the next morning I went up to Mother Teresa after Mass and asked her to pray for him. She told me he would recover. Babloo recovered. Two days later, you would never have known that he almost died.

As soon as we finished prayers that evening, a group of the older and more able children who lived at Shishu came into the chapel to pray. Because the sisters did not have permission for these children to be adopted, the center was their home. In the big room where they lived, they were generally the ringleaders of every activity, but now they were all dressed up as I had never seen them before, and they acted like little adults. For a few moments I watched them as they laid their hearts before God, kneeling at the altar—young contemplatives in the heart of the world.

There is nothing more beautiful than watching children pray. Their innocence and simplicity of faith convicts me. I think this is why Jesus said we must become like little children to enter the kingdom of heaven.

Until I became a Christian, I had no idea how much prayer takes place daily. I have met people who spend hours a day praying for countries, cities, individuals, schools and more. There are many national and international fellowships of intercessors. Some churches, even some campuses, now host prayer vigils twenty-four hours a day, seven days a week. Over a thousand prisoners in a maximum-security prison in Argentina hold all-night prayer vigils for the needs of other inmates and of worldwide ministries they support.[2] There are cities across the globe now where Christians come together from different denominational, racial and economic groups to pray in unity in all-night vigils for the city's needs and authorities. The results are dramatic—decreased crime, increased economic and agricultural production, and increased health and wealth of citizens.[3]

I still have one of Mother's "business cards." It says, "Love to pray—feel often during the day the need for prayer and take trouble to pray. Prayer enlarges the heart until it is capable of containing God's gift of Himself. Ask and seek, and your heart will grow big enough to receive Him and keep Him as your own."

14

The Missionaries and Miracles

THE DAY AFTER BABLOO ALMOST DIED and we had prayed
for him during Adoration, things dramatically turned around. He
began to eat with more vigor, his food stayed in his tiny body and
he gained weight. But there was more to this story than I am really
comfortable telling, which is witness to the power of doubt in the
West and especially in the university regarding the supernatural.

Above the windows facing the crib where Babloo slept that
night—a crib that could hold an IV and a sitting adult if need be—
hung three pictures of Christ. The one on the left was a typical
Sunday school picture depicting the time Jesus told his disciples
to let the little children come to him. It was very colorful. Even
in India, this Christ and the children had soft brown or blonde
hair, probably left over from the British. On the right was another
colorful and iconic picture like those often depicted on Christmas cards where Mary is holding the infant Jesus. The light and
colors in these two pictures were enough to make them attrac-

tive to young eyes. Though by now I had studied Catholicism, become a Benedictine Oblate, attended both Protestant and Catholic churches and was well acquainted with the differences in their symbols, the middle picture still startled me whenever I looked at it. It was a darkly-painted picture, mostly browns, tans and deep reds—a realistic, not iconic, painting of Jesus holding his bleeding heart outside his body in his hand. The heart was brownish red, dripped with blood, had a cross in the top, the crown of thorns and fire wrapped around it.

After his brush with death I lifted Babloo from his crib and began to walk him around. His eyes searched the pictures above the windows until they became fixed upon the picture of the Sacred Heart of Jesus. When Babloo's eyes met this picture, he began to kick excitedly and smile. I thought this odd since this was an unusual reaction of Babloo to anything. His little personality was very calm and unexcitable; despite my valiant attempts, he rarely smiled. I looked at the picture and thought little of it; it was just a coincidence. So I walked him around while I did other things. Yet every time we walked by the windows, he searched out the picture and had the same reaction.

When I was confident that this was a sure thing, I showed some of the sisters, who were very happy about it. Sister Delphinus exclaimed with enthusiasm that this meant Babloo would be a great saint. She had read biographies of saints and had determined that many of them had early responses to icons or pictures of Christ. She herself as a child had sat for hours before a picture of the Sacred Heart of Jesus and contemplated it. I was to learn later that Mother and the Missionaries have a devotion to the Sacred Heart of Jesus. Mother died on the Friday in September when the church honors the Sacred Heart.

All the days that I saw him after that, Babloo maintained his enthusiasm for the picture. Something had happened between

him and Christ that perhaps even he will never consciously remember. A few days later as I held him in front of his favorite
picture he was kicking excitedly and began to coo. For the first
time, Babloo spoke. He gave Jesus a long string of beautiful, sweet
cooing sounds—sounds I had tried to elicit for many weeks to no
avail. The two sufferers, now victors, were communing. Babloo
had passed from near-death into full life.

Now I realize that in the West, one is at risk for reporting such
things and even more at risk for believing in miracles. Certainly
it is not a part of the academy, which even in many religion departments has come up with many alternative explanations for
the miracles of Christ. Nevertheless it happened, and I have seen
other miracles in other places, such as in Argentina where one of
the longest-running, most powerful revivals has been taking place
for over seventeen years.[1] Friends have seen miracles at the ministry of Heidi and Roland Baker[2] in Mozambique where children
from the streets are cared for and adopted. (Heidi often is called
the Protestant Mother Teresa.)

Why are the "developing nations" in Africa and South America
and Asia seeing revivals, signs and wonders so much more than in
the United States or Europe? Why are these events not reported,
researched or discussed in mainstream Western culture? I find
it odd that universities, quick to research anything, do not study
miracles. Essentially, miracles do not fit our prejudices. We tend
to either ignore or discredit anything that does not fit our current
worldview. I am convinced, like many others, that many simply
do not believe the totality of the gospel. We have too little faith—
Mother called it spiritual poverty. Christ proclaimed to many who
were healed, "Your faith has made you well." Many Christians in
economically developed nations do not really believe Christ still
performs miracles, though the Scriptures are full of testimonies,
and the world today is still full of them, even in the disbeliev-

ing West. Universities that teach limited worldviews are partly to blame for this.

C. S. Lewis wrote that a miracle is

> an interference with nature by the supernatural. . . . A miracle is emphatically not an event without cause or without results. Its cause is the activity of God: Its results follow according to Natural law. . . . By definition, miracles must of course interrupt the usual course of Nature; but if they are real they must, in the very act of so doing, assert all the more the unity and self-consistency of total reality at some deeper level.[3]

Theology professor Charles Kraft discusses his problems as a Western missionary in Nigeria:

> Though the Nigerian church leaders decided that a primary strategy would be to focus on God's conquest of the spirits through Christ, I was in no position to assist them. I tried to believe in the reality of evil spirits but I was just plain ignorant in this area. . . . [The Nigerians] learned not to expect power—except in the material realm where we had brought western medicine, schools, agriculture and even a western approach to Christianity—all in the name of Jesus. The Nigerians "knew" that whatever power Christianity brought wasn't adequate to deal with things such as tragedy, infertility, relational breakdowns, and troublesome weather. It [westernized Christianity] didn't meet many of their deepest spiritual needs. . . . We did pray, of course, calmly for ordinary things and fervently when things got really bad. But Western secular techniques were our first choice, God was our last resort. Without meaning to, we taught our African converts that the Christian God works only through western

cultural ways (though they soon learned that our western cultural ways couldn't handle many of their needs).[4]

The Missionaries of Charity relied on the power of God for everything. The sister who had shared the special prayer for Babloo in our campaign to get four ounces of formula in his little body was herself a walking miracle. I came to know her best because she and I fed infants together on the bench. She was from western India and had been serving as a Missionary in the Middle East, I believe, when she began to lose her sight and her ability to speak and walk. Finally it was determined that she had tuberculosis of the brain and was told she was terminally ill. The Missionaries flew her back to Calcutta and she slept on a cot at the Mother House. Instead of dying, she progressively became well. By the time I met her, she could walk and talk and much of her sight had returned.

She was the epitome of the wounded healer.[5] No matter how cranky or ill one of the infants became, we had only to lay them in her lap and all would be well. I used to tease her that after she died, the church would canonize her, and Catholic mothers all over the world would pray for Saint Delphinus's intercession when they could not get their babies to stop crying. She would just smile when I teased her, and I loved to see her smile. She had the face of a young child—pure and full of light—and like all the Missionaries I met, the spirit of a strong and sacrificial woman.

15

If We Say We Have No Sin,
the Truth Is Not in Us

ANOTHER INFANT LIVED AT SHISHU BHAVAN, perhaps five months old, with whom I was much less holy. He was badly deformed and always seemed miserable. Sister Joachim always appeared when it was time to feed him, and to tell the truth, in my heart I was glad. She would draw him very close to her and look at him as though he were the most beautiful child in the world. She would speak to him and touch him as though he was returning her affection, but he never did. If he looked at you, it was always out of misery. When I was near him, I felt I was part of his misery.

One day when feeding time was over, the babies were falling asleep in their bassinets, and I was getting ready to go. I had hung up my cotton apron and was collecting my water bottle from the top of a tall cabinet. I glanced at the infants as I started out and noticed that undigested formula was dripping out of this child's bassinet. He had thrown up what must have been the entire eight-ounce bottle. Looking around quickly for someone to tell as I left, I saw no one in the infant area and the few other adults in the room had their hands full with older children. So I decided, with no little struggle, to stay and clean up the mess. I put on my apron again, lifted the baby out of his bassinet and held him on my shoulder as I began to gather the dirty sheets together and use them to wipe up the mess. As I was cleaning, I heard a muffled sound from the infant in my arm. Tears were pouring out of his eyes and the only sound he could make was a convulsive sob.

As I looked at him, I saw in myself what Jeremiah called the "desperate wickedness of the heart."[1] I realized I had approached this task with a spirit of resistance and impatience. I had thought very little, if at all, about this child and his needs, other than to be clean. As I threw the sheets in the laundry pile, I began to bathe his little misshapen body and change his clothes. Afterward, I held him to me tightly as I had seen Sister Joachim do. I looked at him, rocked him and prayed. I was given the grace in those moments to expect nothing, and I suddenly received something much greater. In a short time, he was asleep. With one arm I found a new sheet, tucked it in the bassinet and laid him down. In those moments I saw this child for the first time as he really was, as the Missionaries saw him—Jesus in the distressing disguise of a poor, lame, hurting child.

I must tell you that the moment I saw him weeping and realized the wretchedness in my heart, I knew it was sin. There was no doubt in my mind that this is what Christ meant when he said, "Out of the heart come evil thoughts."[2] I asked Christ to forgive and change me. In those moments as I rocked the baby, I could feel Christ's work inside of my spirit just as surely as if he were sitting next to me.

G. K. Chesterton remarked that sin is the most empirically provable principle of Christianity, "a fact as practical as potatoes," he called it, and the single principle that causes many to avoid Christ.[3] But with Christ a way is made back to God and away from sin. Confession and forgiveness lead to the grace to love the not-so-loveable, a grace Mother and the Missionaries exploited to the fullest.

Sin is not a common expression these days and just the mention of it can incite anger, even rage, in people. Once I told this story to a group of teachers. For a moment there was silence, broken by a young radical woman who in a loud voice exclaimed that I had hurt her feelings. "Why are you using religious language? Tell us what you have to tell us without it," she exclaimed. After she had gone on for a while, she paused. I pointed out that in the radical theories she had just professed, there is a principle which posits that no knowledge is neutral and that the "secular language" she wanted to hear from me is not neutral either. I explained that I had to tell stories about my own life as I saw them; else, I would be lying to her. I am increasingly convinced that there is no such thing as the secular life. We are all religious in terms of what we believe, whether it is in Christ or Marx.

Ravi Zacharias tells the story of Hobart Mowrer, onetime president of the American Psychological Association, who had written an article in 1960 suggesting that in order to deal with shame and guilt, psychology should reintroduce the concept of sin. He was concerned about the dangers of using the excuse of being sick rather than sinful. Mowrer later said that he received more responses to that comment than to any other he had made in his life. How could an educated psychologist of his stature use such language? In his response, he claimed he was neither a believer nor religious in any way, but that he had recommended the word *sin* because it carries a greater sense of the gravity of the problem. Zacharias points out that Mowrer was pragmatically "smuggling transcendent language" because the secular language lacked enough meaning.[4]

I find no other way to really learn about myself and grow than to remain open to recognizing my sins, confessing them and asking God to cleanse me from them. I find over and over this Scripture proven to be true: "If we confess our sins, he is faithful and just to forgive us our sins and to cleanse us from all unrighteousness."[5] What I cannot do for myself, God surely accomplishes when I confess, ask and yield to his healing power. God not only forgives, he also takes away the unhealthy desires that undergird my sin. Mother Teresa said, "We need humility to acknowledge our sin. The knowledge of our sin helps us to rise. I will get up and go to my Father."[6]

Every morning at Mass and Thursdays at formal confession, the Missionaries look deeply inside themselves for the remaining vestiges of jealousy, greed, anger and other sins, and then confess them. They do not look outside to see the cause of the world's problems; they look inside first. Clarifying what is inside helps to understand what is outside. The heart is only a tiny mirror of the world I so often bemoan.

Correspondent David Aikman described how Aleksandr Solzhenitsyn wrote about sin in the description of his spiritual conversion to Christianity that began on his prison bed. Solzhenitsyn writes in *The Gulag Archipelago*:

> In the intoxication of youthful successes I had felt myself to be infallible, and I was therefore cruel. . . . In my most evil moments I was convinced that I was doing good, and I was well supplied with systematic arguments. And it was only when I lay there on rotting prison straw that I sensed within myself the first stirrings of good. Gradually it was disclosed to me that the line separating good and evil passes not through states, not between classes, nor between political parties either—but right through every human heart—

and through all human hearts. . . . And even in the best of hearts, there remains an unuprooted small corner of evil. . . . It is impossible to expel evil from the world in its entirety, but it is possible to constrict it within each person.[7]

Mother Teresa wrote:

Knowing ourselves puts us in our rightful place. This knowing is necessary for love because the knowledge of God yields love and self-knowledge yields humility. Self-knowledge is very useful. The saints can sincerely say that they are great criminals. They have been able to see God and to see themselves, and they have noted the difference.[8]

She also said,

The true interior life makes the active life burn forth and consume everything. It makes us find Jesus in the dark holes of the slums, in the most pitiful miseries of the poor—the God-Man naked on the cross, mournful, despised by all, the man of suffering crushed like a worm by the scourging and the crucifixion. This interior life motivates the Missionary of Charity to serve Jesus in the poor.[9]

According to Western psychology, Mother Teresa would be described as deeply flawed, guilt-ridden, codependent, depressed, fanatical and even delusional; yet nothing could be further from the truth. Principles of secular psychology are light years from Christian principles and this, too, makes social work and religious work boldly distinct.[10] The world's psychology surrounds us all the time—in grocery store music, TV, movies, in the analyzing of news and everyday conversations. Having become so accustomed to certain ways of thinking, it does not occur to us to challenge it. Denial about the pervasive presence of sin may be the fiercest struggle for a Christian living today in the West.

16

Here God's Grace More Abounds

As A PROFESSOR IN THE SOCIAL SCIENCES, I think I secretly hoped I would find some new theory or method for dealing with the poor that could be applied in classrooms. But I did not find any new method. In fact, the Missionaries do not even use old methods. In the center where I worked, Shishu Bhavan, about fifty children ranging in age from infants to ten-year-olds lived every day in one large room. Apart from a large open area for activities, most of the space was filled with rows of beds. The Missionaries were spread thin, staff was few, and volunteers were sporadic, at best.

Yet the children were happy, contented and well cared for. They enjoyed a consistent schedule for bathing, feeding, playing and sleeping. They laughed as much as other children, if not more. They took care of one another, invented games and took full advantage of the young, energetic volunteers, getting rides on their backs and incorporating them into their antics. In any other room with that many children of that many ages with that range of abilities and disabilities, and so little in the way of coordinated activities, chaos would have reigned. But not here.

One day I asked Sister Bethany, one of the lovely sisters in charge of volunteers, how she explained the absence of chaos at these centers. She smiled and answered, "Where there is poverty and oppression, there the grace of God more abounds."[1] You could almost feel the lightness and fluidity of God's grace on these children and the sisters. With all the prayer and humility, the work went unfettered by despair; the place ran smoothly and joyfully.

To the Missionaries, the poor, the sick and the handicapped offered the rest of us opportunities to demonstrate the love and power of God. Mother Teresa and her sisters exploited fully the abundant grace of God. They believed in it, thanked God for it, received it and put it to use.

Perhaps this is another reason why so many more healings and miracles are manifested in places of great poverty and need—the grace of God flourishes amidst oppression. By necessity the poor live closer to nature and are more aware of the spiritual reality that lies behind the natural. Most do not debate the existence of good and evil—they know it. And unlike my earlier, naive version of "spirituality," they know that *spiritual* is not synonymous with *good*; spiritual forces may be good or evil, healthy or destructive. Knowing the difference takes spiritual discernment, as surface features are often deceptive.

For the Missionaries of Charity and much of the economically developing world, faith rests first in God's power and second in human invention. As theologian Charles Kraft points out in discussing the denial of Christ's power in the West:

> It is interesting (and discouraging) to note that even though we are Christians, our basic assumptions are usually more like those of non-Christian westerners around us than we

like to admit. We have as Christians, made certain modifications. But even though there is often a wide discrepancy between the teachings of Scripture and the common Western assumptions . . . we often find ourselves more Western than Scriptural. . . . This tension is especially acute if we seek to be more open in the area of spiritual power.[2]

I began to wonder how things would be different if all of us who work with the poor, materially or spiritually, followed the Missionaries' examples to fully realize the grace of God through prayer, obedience, chastity, confession, diligence and perseverance. What kind of power might that yield for true disciples of Christ inside or outside of the convent?

17

Sometimes We Get Lost
When We Look at Numbers

✺

MOTHER TOLD OF A TIME WHEN SHE spoke at a conference on
world hunger in Bombay. "I was supposed to go to that meeting and I lost the way. Suddenly I came to that place, and right
in front of the door to where hundreds of people were talking
about food and hunger, I found a dying man, I took him out and I
took him home. He died there. He died of hunger. And the people
inside were talking about how in fifteen years we will have so
much food, so much this, so much that, and that man died. See
the difference?"[1]

Politically minded intellectuals often criticized Mother Teresa
for not getting involved in the politics of poverty, for speaking
out against abortion and for feeding the poor directly rather than
"teaching them to fish." However, Mother Teresa was not what
you could call a political woman. She told Muggeridge,

If there are people who feel that God wants them to change the structures of society, that is something between them and God. We must serve him in whatever way we are called. I am called to help the individual; to love each poor person. Not to deal with institutions. I am in no position to judge. . . . All of us are but his instruments, who do our little bit and pass by.[2]

She believed that "welfare is for a purpose—an admirable one— whereas Christian love is for a person."[3]

She said she was a very simple woman who had only been called to feed, clothe, bathe and tend the poorest of the poor. If she tried to do things outside of her calling, she would be less effective in the "little things" God had given her to do. She did not have a political or economic analysis of poverty. Her complete assessment was "God does not create poverty; it is created by you and I because we don't share."[4] Yet she did work with governments and church authorities. For example, the mayor of Calcutta had an open door policy one morning a week. Mother would stand in line with the poor to urge him to fix a sewer or broken water pipe in a poor neighborhood. She said that she herself did not agree with the

big way of doing things. To us what matters is an individual. To get to love the person we must come in close contact with him. If we wait until we get the numbers, then we will be lost in the numbers. And we will never be able to show that love and respect for the person. I believe in person to person; every person is Christ for me, and since there is only one Jesus, that person is only one person in the world for me at that moment. . . . In these times of development, everybody is in a hurry and everybody's in a rush, and on the way there are people falling down, who are not able to compete. These are the ones we want to love and serve and take care of.[5]

She said they worked one person at a time, "one, one, one, one" she would tell us, then you would find you had picked up 40,000 people from the streets. They worked with people that other agencies did not serve.

The humility and clarity with which Mother Teresa understood her task in life was one of the most incredible things about her. People go into teaching, nursing, politics or business with ideas of doing revolutionary things. I once encouraged this unrealistic zeal in my students who became teachers. Now I see how easily they became depressed and discouraged. Moreover, the "little things" they actually did in their classrooms—which were big things for individual children—could be overlooked amidst an emphasis on, for example, system-wide school restructuring. Starting out with fervor to change the world can be a quick route to discouragement. Sometimes despair is a result of thinking too highly of oneself, other times too little. Wrong thinking, poor attitudes and misguided motivations sabotage the work. Soon the real calling is lost, and no one has the grace or skills to work outside their calling.

Mother Teresa's ability to avoid this stultifying despair was because of her incredible humility and the single-mindedness with which she approached her calling. Nothing could sway her from what God had called her to do. If there was one characteristic of hers I desire, it was her ability to know and to focus on her life's purpose. She did not become confused, distracted or discouraged by criticisms or complements. She remained able to hear clearly and respond immediately to the voice of God. Although I've heard of not letting critics pull us off our call, I forget that people who mean well can do the same. Jesus was also cautious about those who believed in him: "Now when he was in Jerusalem at the Passover Feast, many believed in his name when they saw the signs that he was doing. But Jesus on his part did not entrust himself to them, because he knew all people and needed no one to bear witness about man, for he himself knew what was in man."[6]

Mother said, "There should be less talk; a preaching point is not a meeting point. What do you do then? Take a broom and clean someone's house. That says enough."[7] In a note she wrote to me after I mailed her a small, beginning piece of this manuscript, she called their work "little nothingness."

18

Don't Give In
to Discouragement

❧❧

MOTHER TERESA FREQUENTLY CALLED the work "just a
drop in the ocean. But if that drop was not in the ocean, I think
the ocean would be less."[1] Mother wrote to the sisters, "Don't give
in to discouragement. No more must you do so when you try to
settle a marriage crisis or convert a sinner and don't succeed. If
you are discouraged, it is a sign of pride because it shows you
trust in your own powers. Never bother about people's opinion.
Be humble and you will never be disturbed. It is very difficult to
practice because we all want to see the result of our work. Leave
it to Jesus."[2]

Muggeridge analyzed the work this way:

It is perfectly true, of course, that, statistically speaking,
what [Mother] achieves is little, or even negligible. But then
Christianity is not a statistical view of life. That there should

be more joy in heaven over one sinner who repents than over all the hosts of the just is an anti-statistical proposition. God is fond throughout the Hebrew and Greek Scriptures of doing much with little. He even sent home most of Gideon's army to win a war. He says He uses the simple to confound the wise, and the despised to become mighty.[3]

I never heard a Missionary of Charity discussing how to rid the world of poverty. No one wrung their hands over the fact that many needy people on the streets of Calcutta went untouched by the work of these few hundred women. The sisters simply took in the poorest of the poor, those least likely to get other help. I remember one day chatting with Mother on a bench while I waited to pick up some materials at the Mother House. She was enthusiastically discussing a new work to get prostitutes out of jail and put them in a house and teach them skills so that they could get jobs. Anything could grant the sisters great encouragement and gratitude—a toddler's first step, a child's temperature lowering or a person eating their first meal in a long time.

Because of the popular English name of the most well-known center, The Home for the Dying, many believed that people died there all the time; but this was not the case. The volunteers who worked there when I was there said that rarely did more than one or two out of a hundred die in a week.

At Shishu, only one child died in the two months I was there. He died shortly after arriving, having been burned badly in a fire set by his father to get rid of his wife and children. The mother died; the other son lived and stayed at Shishu the entire time I worked there. The extended family was deciding whether to take him or give him up. None of this horror deterred the Missionaries. Mother forbade them from giving into despair; she kept them focused on Jesus and doing the work at hand. They seemed to all know exactly why they were there and to what they had been called. "Do our best, that's all God asks, but He does ask for our best."

It is not that Mother never had feelings of discouragement, but she never gave in. She never stopped her faithfulness, her prayer or her work. She confessed her discouragements to her confessors, asked them for prayer and God for his help, and returned swiftly to the truths of the gospel and to leading her contemplatives in the heart of the world.

What I cannot change or what lies ahead easily overwhelms me. What lies behind can be overwhelming as well. Perhaps it is an occupational hazard, but my mind is so full of utopian philosophies and theories that it constantly struggles to focus on the reality of human nature and to stay grounded in what can be done immediately. However, the Missionaries live the life that Jesus commanded when he said, "Therefore do not be anxious about tomorrow, for tomorrow will be anxious for itself. Sufficient for the day is its own trouble."[4] They gave things over to God who could make small things big and big problems small. While with the Missionaries, I learned the satisfaction and joy of meeting a simple need and moving on to meet the next one.

Theophan the Recluse, a nineteenth-century Orthodox saint, corresponded with people to mentor them in their spiritual lives. His letters to one young woman have been preserved. In several of these letters, he addressed a problem that he called "progressivism." The young woman suddenly expressed confusion about her purpose in life, a concern that had apparently not surfaced in her previous letters, and he writes the following:

> I would guess that among your friends are progressive thinkers, or that you have joined a society having such people in it, and they have scattered your good sense. Such people usually rave in this manner. Phrases such as "the

good of mankind" and "the good of the people" are always on their tongues. . . . The progressives have in mind all mankind or at least all of its people lumped together. The fact is, however, that "mankind" or "the people" does not exist as a person for whom you could do something right now. It consists of individual persons: By doing something for one person, we are doing it within the general mass of humanity. If each one of us did what was possible to do for whoever was standing right in front of our eyes, instead of goggling at the community of mankind, then all people, in aggregate, would at each moment be doing that which is needed by those in need, and, by satisfying their needs, would establish the welfare of all mankind, which is made up of haves and have-nots, the weak and the strong. But those who keep thoughts of the welfare of all mankind inattentively let slip by that which is in front of their eyes. Because they do not have the opportunity to perform a particular work, they accomplish nothing towards the main purpose of life.[5]

Theophan goes on to tell the young woman a story of a well-known "progressive" in St. Petersburg who, having just made an impassioned speech about the love of all mankind, goes home and strikes his servant in the chest for not responding to his needs with enough haste. He concludes the letter: "All troubles come from a mental outlook that is too broad. It is better to cast your eyes down toward your feet, and to figure out which step to take where. This is the truest path. . . . I am guarding you from the obfuscation that progressivist's dreams direct at the soul."[6] Thomas Merton wrote, "There are plenty of men who will give up their interests for the sake of 'society,' but cannot stand any of the people they live with."[7]

This is the problem of utopian visions: they stir up intense dissatisfaction, anger and even violence because with human nature they are not realizable. These visions are devastating when the utopian leader is evil and wields great power, such as in the case of Hitler, Stalin, Lenin, Mao, Pol Pot and Kim. Such tyrants must oppress more and more in order to hide the lie of the utopian vision.

Mother Teresa addressed the members of a Eucharistic Conference in 1976 and told the following story.

I saw a young boy with beautiful long hair sitting at night in the street. I said to him, "You shouldn't be here. You should be with your parents. This is not the place for you to be sitting in this cold night." He looked straight into my eyes and said, "My mother doesn't want me because I have long hair." That was all. I reflected for a second that it was quite possible that his mother was very busy with the hunger of India and Africa and all these places. She wanted to feed everybody except her own child. She did not know that the poverty of hunger was in her own home and she was the cause of that hunger. This is why I ask, do we really know our poor? Do we know how poor we are?[8]

19

Mother Teresa's
Dark Night of the Spirit

As a deer pants for flowing streams,
So pants my soul for you, O God.

PSALM 42:1

THE EVIDENCE OF MOTHER TERESA'S longing to feel the presence
of the Lord is everywhere in her writings, not just in the letters
revealed after her death in the book *Come Be My Light,* edited by
Brian Kolodiejchuk.[1] To me, the letters matched the fathomless,
otherworldly longing always present in her eyes, even when she
was smiling. When I was there, I felt the thing that most revealed
the secret behind that look was the phrase emblazoned on the
wall next to the crucifix in every one of her order's chapels worldwide: I thirst. Jesus was thirsting for the souls of the poorest of
the poor; Mother was thirsting for more of him. In 1980 she wrote
to one of her confessors,[2] "I do not know whose Thirst is greater,
His or mine for Him."[3]

Much of her writing reads like an instruction manual on ways to suffer redemptively. Take for example, this piece from a letter to the sisters:

> My dear children, without our suffering, our work would just be social work, very good and helpful, but it would not be the work of Jesus Christ, not part of the redemption, Jesus wanted to help us by sharing our life, our loneliness, our agony and death. All that He has taken upon Himself, He has carried it in the darkest night, only by being one with us has he redeemed us. We are allowed to do the same, all the desolation of the poor people, not only their material poverty, but also their spiritual destitution, must be redeemed and we must share in it."[4]

Such words resemble Paul's to the Galatians, "My little children, for whom I am again in the anguish of childbirth until Christ is formed in you!"[5]

It is important at the outset of discussing Mother's dark nights to understand that while some popular media have focused their reviews of the book on what they call her "crisis of faith," the truth is that in over three hundred pages, the majority of which are her letters, there are only two lines where she questions her faith. Mother began and ended even these two letters with a loving resignation to God. Primarily in these letters, which began after the establishment of the Missionaries of Charity, Mother shares with her confessors her longing for more of Christ and her feelings of his absence. In probably the most painful letter, often partially quoted, she says,

> Where is my faith?—even deep down . . . there is nothing but emptiness and darkness. . . . I have no faith. . . . So many unanswered questions live within me—I am afraid to uncover

them—because of blasphemy—If there be God,—please forgive me. . . . Did I make the mistake of surrendering blindly
to the call of the Sacred Heart? The work is not a doubt—
because I am convinced that it is His not mine . . . not even a
single simple thought or temptation enters my heart to claim
anything in the work. . . . In spite of all—this darkness and
emptiness is not as painful as the longing for God. . . . What
are you doing My God to one so small?

Mother ends the letter:

If this brings You glory, . . . if my suffering satiates Your
Thirst—here I am Lord, with joy I accept all to the end of
life—and I will smile at Your Hidden Face—always.[6]

These are hardly the words of someone contemplating atheism. She also wrote that somehow God was using this darkness
to break through and that through it all, she felt a presence of
"somebody living inside her."[7] I believe the Holy Spirit so freely
operated through her that Christ's presence became less distinct
from her own. She no longer needed him to speak to her in visions
and words; she had the mind of Christ.[8]

The larger context is this: Mother had any number of mystical
experiences with Christ during her early years and prior to the
founding of the Missionaries. On numerous occasions she heard
the voice of Jesus asking her to go into the dark holes of the poorest and be his light, to establish an order of Indian nuns, and to be
his "little spouse." In addition to hearing his voice, she had three
mystical visions of Christ speaking to her from the cross. But
these disappeared as the Missionaries were formally established.

Across the ages, great saints have gone through similar trials.
After the mystical experiences with Christ disappear, they are
plunged into excruciating purgation. Teresa of Ávila, author of

the classic work on prayer *The Interior Castle,* endured eighteen years of dryness, saying the prayers of the church with her mouth but not with her heart. Bonaventure described these dark nights as the experience of diving into God's darkness where one only experiences the silence of God. The trials of Job, David, Paul and Peter and all the prophets, poets, kings, philosophers and fishermen who wrote the books that became the Bible testify to periods of "downcast souls" when they "despaired of life itself."

John of the Cross wrote that the dark night of the soul was often a prelude to a much darker night—the night of the spirit. This seems to have been Mother's path. He writes: "They harbor in the midst of the dryness and emptiness of their faculties, a habitual care and solitude for God accompanied by grief or fear about not serving Him. It is a sacrifice most pleasing to God—that of a spirit in distress and solicitude for his love. . . . it begins to kindle in the spirit divine love."[9]

First, Mother did fear in the beginning of her dark nights that she was not serving God well. She pleads with her confessors to pray that she not refuse Jesus. She once asked Pope John Paul II to pray that she not spoil the work, to which he replied, "And you, Mother, pray I may not spoil the Church."[10]

Second, to do what Mother did—indeed, what the Missionaries do—she had to have his divine love. No other love (not *agape,* not *eros,* not *philia*[11]) could sustain the work with the poorest of the poor in the conditions in which they live. Saint Francis de Sales, of the early seventeenth century, described divine love as making "its abode in the most high and sublime region of the soul, where it offers sacrifices."[12] All of us who really experienced working with her and the Missionaries, even for short periods, know in our hearts that we could not have maintained it. This love was a love born of surrender, loss and God's grace. Mother said, "The less we have, the more we give. Seems absurd, but it's the logic of love."[13]

When the glorious mystical experiences ended and a dark night began, I suspect I would have slowed my pursuit of God. Mother seems to have used it as a reason to increase her efforts. Kolodiejchuk says, "Instead of stifling her missionary impulse, the darkness seemed to invigorate it."[14]

From her early life with Christ, Mother prayed for three things: to be a saint (humble and meek), to share in his passion and not to refuse him anything. God granted her all three.

Still, the revelation of her inner emptiness strikes terror in the hearts of those who continue to press into God for the high calling. In one of Mother's letters she said,

> I do not know how much deeper will this trial go—how much pain and suffering it will bring to me.—This does not worry me any more. I leave this to Him as I leave everything else. I want to become a saint according to the Heart of Jesus—meek and humble. That is all that really matters to me now.[15]

This is why, by the time she received the Nobel Prize and other awards, they meant nothing to her. She accepted them in the name of Jesus and the poor and kept them closed up in a cupboard. She wrote, "I want Him, not His gifts or creatures."[16] It brought her soul no refreshment, for God's spirit, working in her, dominated her soul. She longed for God alone. She begged Pope John Paul II to release her from the demands of the world to travel and speak and permit her to just stay with her sisters and the poor. He believed she was called to minister to both. She accepted. We can only imagine what a different woman she would have been if she had begun to love the prizes and adulations of men and women, while living from one spiritual high to the next.

God thus protected Mother from the pride that would have prevented her from one of the graces she had begged him to give her and her sisters—to be saints. Father Scolozzi writes:

She said to her Sisters, "I will not be satisfied if you are just good religious [nuns]. I want to be able to offer God a perfect sacrifice. To resolve to be a saint means I will despoil myself of all that is not God." Her aim for herself and those in her care is perfection, not the kind that comes from self-striving, but the true holiness of life that comes from total dedication to Jesus and abandonment to His purposes.[17]

God also gave Mother Teresa the second grace for which she fervently prayed—to share in the passion of Christ, "to drink ONLY from His chalice of pain."[18] Again the Lord was gracious, arranging for her to have a few confessors who apparently completely understood that through her emptiness she actually was sharing in the passion of Christ and the sufferings of the poor. She was filling up what was lacking in Christ's suffering for the poorest of the poor. Paul described the same suffering, "Now I rejoice in my sufferings for your sake, and in my flesh I am filling up what is lacking in Christ's afflictions for the sake of his body, that is, the church."[19] Mother wrote to her sisters, "Keep giving Jesus to your people. . . . Accept whatever he gives—and give whatever he takes with a big smile. You belong to him. Tell him: 'I am yours, and if you cut me to pieces, every single piece will be only all yours.'"[20]

God gives many promises, and Christians are quick to display some of them on coffee cups. However, one of the promises of God we are not so quick to celebrate is the promise of suffering. A quick glance at a concordance under the words *suffer, suffering* and *suffered* reveal these promises. Contemplate these words of Peter in the context of Mother's life: "Therefore let those who suffer according to God's will entrust their souls to a faithful Creator while doing good."[21] And the words of Mother to a confessor who had advised her, "For the first time in this 11 years—I have come to love the darkness—for I believe now that it is a part of a very,

very small part of Jesus' darkness and pain on earth. You have taught me to accept it as a 'spiritual side of your work.'"[22]

Across the ages, devout people have understood the price of answering God's highest call. They have told us for centuries that mystical desserts often turn into deserts. These mystical delights, in the words of Joy Dawson, "forever ruin us for the ordinary."[23] They tend to disappear as one is called into deeper levels of spiritual maturity and higher levels of service to God and humanity. John of the Cross and others provide a brilliant analysis of the spiritual dark night, but faithful to her own experience, Mother's letters reveal the painful reality of dark nights grounded in ordinary existence.

We have a hard time in the West (and perhaps especially among Protestants) getting our heads around these spiritual realities because somewhere in the early Middle Ages, the mystics were no longer welcomed in universities and seminaries, or to be advisers in governments, businesses, hospitals and other institutions. The mystics were relegated to monasteries and the scholastics to the university. The mystics' wisdom is all but lost. Many Christians, like myself, struggle because we also live primarily by naturalism and humanism—we grope along by sight and feel.

Even Christians may tend to analyze Mother as depressed and wonder if it would not have been better for her to take Prozac. Sadly, much Christian counseling today, even in churches, is little more than secular psychology sandwiched between a beginning and ending prayer. It's a desperate attempt to avoid and appease suffering. However, not one iota of this psychology colors Mother's writings; it simply was not a part of her worldview. Had her dark night been psychological depression, she would have been negative, resentful, hopeless, anxious, and have lacked energy and focus.[24] We would have avoided rather than run to her.

Jesus tells us there is only one test of discipleship—the fruit. The only test we have to determine whether her dark night was from God and whether she endured it in a godly manner is, did her life result in bringing glory and honor to Jesus? Did her darkness produce light? Yes! And this not only for those she directly served, but also for those like me who went looking for something that we could not even articulate.

Father Scolozzi writes:

> I believed Mother could provide answers to many of the questions that characterized my own spiritual journey. Instead, I learned that her invitation simply led to more questions, until finally I reached the ultimate ones. I had to face the agony of losing and finding myself in total surrender to the One who knows why we must be buried in the death of his Son before we can rise to a newness of life. I began to realize that no one can effectively serve God's poor without first breaking out of the prison of his own ego. Mother told me it takes a lot of humiliation to produce just a little bit of humility.[25]

Mother described her life and the lives of the Missionaries as a sacrifice to God that made reparation for the sins of the world—their chastity for our immorality, their poverty for our materialism, their obedience for our rebellion, their free service to the poor for our greed. And I would add: her spiritual darkness for our godlessness. Like Jesus, Mother became "numbered with the transgressors,"[26] her spiritual emptiness made reparation for our abandonment of God and the poorest of the poor.

Despite her feelings of emptiness, Mother Teresa was full. Despite her feelings of darkness, she radiated the light of Christ. The presence of Christ was tangible when you entered her presence. People came from all over the world and from all walks of life just to touch her and have her touch them and their babies, born and unborn.

Every ounce of Jesus that flowed continuously and purely through her, Mother gave away to those of us who came with only our poverty.

20

The Humor of Mother Teresa

⊰⊱

MOTHER TERESA'S ONLY BROTHER, Lazarus, is quoted as saying that Mother had a slightly impish way about her. "She was no goody, goody," he said.[1] I saw this side of Mother several times. The most poignant example was when I sat on a bench talking to her and asked if I could take her picture (with my fancy Kodak disposable). She said, "Yes, because I have a deal with God." Taken aback, I asked what sort of deal that might be, and she answered that for every picture taken of her, she got to send another poor person to heaven. Soon heaven would be full of the poor. She said she had a dream one day during a fever that she saw St. Peter at the gate of heaven. He told her to go back because there were no slums in heaven. Therefore, she needed to fill heaven with people from the slums so she could get in.

Father Angelo tells the story of his accompanying her to see Pope John Paul II. As they went through the rooms of the Vatican on their way to meet him, Mother stopped in each one and took a long look around. When they got to the waiting area, Mother turned to him and said, "Brother, do you remember what I was going to ask the Holy Father?" Father Angelo replied, "Mother, how could you forget why you had come?" She said, "Brother, did you see all the poor outside the Vatican and all those rooms; I was counting how many beds I could get in there." Soon afterward, the Pope arranged for a large home and chapel for the Missionaries on the edge of the Vatican.[2]

Father Angelo, who looks as much like Santa Claus as anyone I have ever met, once asked Mother to give him a spiritual name. She said, "Brother Lamba Chul," which means "Long Hair." Ultimately, she did also give him the name Devananda or "Blissful Angel."

When Pope John Paul II visited Calcutta and was ready to leave, Mother arranged for the Calcutta police to escort his entourage to the airport via a route that passed several of her centers. The people stood outside waving to him as in a parade. The Pope's consort radioed to the Calcutta motorcycle police to protest that they were not taking the route they had given them. One of the officers answered back, "This is the route that Mother Teresa gave us; here in Calcutta we take our orders from Mother." The Pope was amused; his consort apparently not so.[3]

Pope Paul VI gave her the white Lincoln car, which had been given to him by a benefactor, to use at a Eucharistic Conference in Bombay in 1964. Mother promptly raffled it off—for over seven times its value—for the poor.[4] The sisters were concerned she would do the same with her awards.

She also once volunteered the young women in one of the homes for prostitutes to a film crew seeking to film people praying in the middle of the night on the World Day of Prayer. Jaime Cardinal Sin, archbishop of Manila, was to lead the prayer at midnight in the Philippines. She told the producer, "We recently opened a

house for rehabilitation of prostitutes in a suburb of Manila. . . .
It will be wonderful to have Cardinal Sin with our Sisters and our
ex-prostitutes, all praying together. Midnight is the time at which
they are accustomed to work."[5]

One of the requirements to be a Missionary of Charity is to
smile. Mother believed that their smiles helped lighten the sadness
of the poor. "Our poor people suffer much, and unless we go with
joy we cannot help them. We will make them more miserable."[6]
The sisters shared Mother's humor. I remember Sister Delphinus
and others at Shishu would playfully try to guess what each baby
would do in their lives from their emerging little personalities.
We apparently had little future politicians, teachers, construction
workers and, of course, one saint in our nursery.

Mother said at the Eucharistic Conference in 1976, "I remember some professors came to our house. They asked, 'Tell us
something, Mother, that will change our lives.' I said, 'Smile at
each other.' One of them asked me, 'Are you married?' And I said,
'Yes. I find it's sometimes very difficult to smile at Jesus: He can
be very demanding.'"[7]

21

Spreading the Fragrance of Christ

﹥﹤

ONE MORNING AS I FOLLOWED Mother Teresa out of Mass, I noticed she reached down to pick up a tissue and then a piece of paper lying on the floor ahead of her. If you follow the Missionaries of Charity for long, you will find that in their wake everything is left better, whether by their actions or simply their smiles and prayers. One of the sisters at Shishu carried a rag everywhere. She went along wiping and dusting as she stood over cribs and prayed. She would clean little faces, straighten bedclothes, pick up trash or return misplaced items. Mother Teresa called this "spreading the fragrance of Christ."

Evangelical Christians often criticized Mother for not being more active in converting people to Christianity. But at the time when Mother was developing her work, the Catholic church was strictly forbidden from evangelizing in India. It was the condition given the Catholic church in order to remain in India after the British had been expelled. Mother could easily have been deported if she had proselytized. However, Mother was called to evangelism.

One of the Missionaries' major goals is to bring Christ to the people and the people to Christ. Much of their evangelism is to simply show people Jesus in action. Father Angelo told me that when people would ask Mother Teresa to do many different things, she would say to him, "Remember, brother, I am a missionary and so are you." She believed people would be drawn to know this Jesus if they could see him in action. Mother's successor, Sister Nirmala Joshi, MC, a Hindu of the highest caste, converted to Christianity because she saw the truth of Christ in the life of Mother. (Though she herself refuses to be called "Mother," indicating that the Missionaries have only one Mother.) Many opportunities arose for the Missionaries to present Christ directly since people were curious when the sisters acted like Christ.

Mother Teresa insisted that the Missionaries spread the fragrance of Christ. They always bowed their heads and folded their hands toward people they passed on the street in a sign of blessing and respect. Mother told the sisters, "Let no one ever come to you without leaving better and happier." Cardinal Newman's prayer was one of the prayers that we recited every morning after Mass and before going out to the centers. It was written on the prayer card that the Missionaries gave us as a gift when we left.

Dear Jesus, help us to spread your fragrance everywhere we go. Flood our souls with your spirit and life. Penetrate and possess our whole being, so utterly, that our lives may only be a radiance of yours. Shine through us, and be so in us, that every soul we come in contact with may feel your presence in our soul. Let them look up and see no longer us but only Jesus! Stay with us, and then we shall begin to shine as you shine; so to shine as to be a light to others; the light O Jesus, will be all from you, none of it will be ours; it will be you, shining on others through us. Let us thus praise you in the way you love best by shining on those around us. Let us preach you without preaching, not by words but by our example. By the catching force, the sympathetic influence of what we do, the evident fullness of the love our heart bears to you. Amen.

I have thought how much our culture would benefit from an increase in intentional (not random) acts of kindness, gratitude and obedience. I will never forget hearing Joyce Meyer talk about the importance of returning shopping carts to their proper place. She told a story of how the Holy Spirit asked her to hang up some clothes that had fallen off a store rack and the funny way she argued with the Holy Spirit, to no avail, that she had not caused them to fall.[1] Ever since, my best friend, Sandra, and I cannot leave the cart anywhere but in its designated place, and we often hang up things that have fallen off racks.

Driving in Los Angeles, I often think of drivers on the two-lane roads where I grew up in Texas who would pull over to the side to let a faster car by and how the recipient of the grace would give a big wave. We could use a lot more grace and friendly waves of gratitude on the freeways. I have a friend whose example taught me to wipe up the sink and even use my paper to pick up other paper in public restrooms. I noted yesterday a young man throwing trash on the street at our complex. I remembered how my lovely ninety-seven-year-old neighbor, Irene, on her daily walks, used to pick up paper and trash in the alleys as she pushed her walker. We have so many opportunities to leave things better every day.

22

It Matters Not, He Is Forgiven

ONE DAY WHILE SITTING WITH MOTHER TERESA on a bench outside her office, she told a priest and me that some Hindu students had just brought her some money. She mentioned a fund for special relief work—the sisters affectionately called it "Mother's Little Bank." They saved the money from fasting on the first Friday of every month, and other change like this donation from the students, for poor people's emergencies. That is how they started the work to get prostitutes out of jail and help prepare them to enter the job market. I had read that the sisters actually did not fast because they lived each day like the poor, so I asked her about it. She explained that in the beginning they did not, but now did, and that they save the money for special needs.

At that time, I had just finished reading Christopher Hitchens's very critical book.[1] I knew Mother Teresa knew of it because in the book it states that she was asked to comment on its predecessor, a BBC film. In addition to accusing her of taking money from questionable characters, the book portrays Mother as a woman stingily controlling large sums of money. So I said to her, "Mother, there are people who write books about you who say that you do not need any more money." She looked at me quizzically at first, then in recognition said, "Oh, the book. Yes, well, I haven't read it all, but I know it. Some of the sisters have read it. Ask them. It matters not, he is forgiven." I pushed her one step further and told her that when the author learned that she had said this, it sent him into quite a rage. He said he did not ask for or need her forgiveness. She replied as though I had not understood. "Oh, it is not I that forgives; it is God. God forgives. God has forgiven." Mother Teresa asked me to bring her a copy of the book. I never did.

Forgiveness is one of the essential principles of Christianity if one is to live fully and have any hope of fulfilling one's destiny. Otherwise bitterness consumes the spirit and makes the work more arduous, less joyful. Argentinean pastor Ed Silvoso points out that forgiveness is not an emotion; it is an act of the will.[2] As we pray and claim with our wills our decision to forgive, God grants us the grace that makes forgiving even the unforgiveable possible. Forgiveness frees us. Unforgiveness is a relentless enemy to all who hold onto it. Pastor Che Ahn says that holding onto unforgiveness is like drinking poison and hoping the other person will die.[3] In probably the best book on forgiveness that I have read, R. T. Kendall points out that until we can pray in earnest that God will bless the person who hurt us, we have not fully forgiven.[4]

Mother told many stories of helping people to forgive and be forgiven. Early in her work, she picked up a very bitter and ill woman who railed about her son having thrown her into the streets years before. As Mother bathed her, she urged her to forgive. The woman did, and died in peace a few hours later.[5]

In the Missionaries' home for alcoholics in Melbourne, Australia, a man the sisters were tending had been badly beaten. When the police arrived, the man lied, saying that he did not know the identity of the person who had beaten him. When the police left, the sisters asked him why he had lied. "His suffering is not going to lessen my suffering,"[6] the man replied.

The Missionaries often go to help in refugee camps around the world. Mother said that while they can relieve some of the physical suffering, still there can never be peace without forgiveness.[7] During the Beirut war, Mother rescued a group of Arab handicapped children. Then she spoke to the political leaders urging them not only to forgive, but also to ask for forgiveness. She said it took a great deal of humility to forgive and even more to ask for forgiveness.[8] Theologian Lewis Smedes said that every true act of forgiveness is a miracle.[9] Mother said, "Forgiveness is a decision which starts the process of healing."[10]

After I finished Hitchens's derogatory book about Mother Teresa, I did speak with some sisters. One of them recounted that when she spoke to Mother about how terrible it was, Mother said, "Jesus suffered so much. We must share in his sufferings." The sister said, "She is right; we have so little sufferings." Mother often told the sisters when they faced special trials, "You know, this is a chance for greater love."[11]

Another told me that a group of sisters agreed to read the book and then met together in fasting and prayer. They passed the book around and read it one by one, praying all the while. Then one Thursday, they gathered together and sought God for the purpose of the book for them. When I asked what they had determined, she exclaimed with great delight, "Oh, the book is a call for us to become more holy!" Another sister standing with us said smiling, "Yes, it is to help us become more holy."

Mother Teresa wrote to her sisters in 1963:

We must become holy, not because we want to feel holy, but because Christ must be able to live his life fully in us. Let Christ radiate and live His life in you and through you in the slums. Let the poor, seeing you, be drawn to Christ and invite Him to enter their homes and their lives. Let the sick and suffering find in you a real angel of comfort and consolation. Let the little ones of the streets cling to you because you remind them of Him, the friend of the little ones.[12]

Well, their response to the critical book was very different from mine. At first, the book made me furious. I was angry not only at the author's arrogance, but even more at his ignorance about which he wrote. It was clear in this and other works by Hitchens that he lacks categories in his worldview which can handle what he witnessed, and he has yet to open his mind to other possibilities. Nevertheless, I was to realize what the book of James in the Bible teaches—that human anger does not produce the justice or righteousness of God.

As the fog was lifted from my mind, I began to see how the fundamental principles of life with Christ were so the opposite of my own automatic ways of thinking, being and reacting. I realized that to live a Christian life, I would have to live it upside-down or inside-out from all I had known before.

The sisters had listened to God and found the way to turn this humiliation into greater humility and the suffering into holiness. Mother Teresa reminded us, "When someone is doing something to hurt you, don't turn inward, turn toward that person. He is hurting himself. You must learn to forgive, knowing that we all need forgiveness. If you want to be true to God, you must learn from Jesus to be meek, humble, and pure."[13]

23

Fighting Abortion with Adoption

THE CHILDREN'S CENTERS RUN BY the Missionaries of Charity take in unwanted children and match them with adoptive parents. Mother Teresa said they fought abortion by adoption. Every life, including the unborn, was sacred to her. She adamantly opposed abortion and begged people to give her unwanted infants and she would take care of them. In the United States alone, approximately 4,000 abortions occur each day, and now professionals are discovering the potential physical and psychological consequences to the mother.[1]

I know this reality personally as I had two abortions in my twenties. When I began to follow Christ, I grew deeply remorseful. I know there have been problems in my body, soul and spirit that directly relate to those decisions. For a couple of years after my conversion to Christianity, I repented over and over, unsure whether God could really forgive me for what I now knew as grievous sin. One day at a monastery during a retreat on healing the family tree, Father Sam assigned us to write on a piece of paper the things we needed to repent of and the people we were committing to forgive. We would burn the paper after an evening service as a prayer, an oblation to God.

At the head of my list were my two abortions. I put it in my pocket and began to walk along the Pecos River that runs by the monastery. All at once I heard a male voice in my spirit clearly say, "Who are you not to forgive someone I have forgiven?" I stopped, stunned and confused by the question that had appeared in my spirit. Not understanding, I walked further and the same question came again. I looked at my list and started forward when the voice occurred yet again. Then I stopped and said aloud, "Lord, who have I not forgiven?" Into my spirit the Lord spoke, "I forgave you the first time you asked me. I do not want you to ask me again."

I had learned it is necessary to confess in order to be forgiven; but I had not yet learned how critical it is to intentionally receive his free gift of forgiveness. My pride was waiting until I was satisfied that I had worked hard enough to deserve this free gift from God. I was assigning myself my own endless acts of penance—repeating rituals of naming my children, confessing the same sin over and over, thinking I needed to remain remorseful, and expecting punishment. Once we are forgiven, God calls us to leave the past behind and press on toward our calling. Not doing so is the work of evil trying to block our destiny.

Many people talk about the need to forgive ourselves, but that is not what the Lord was saying to me. I believe working to forgive ourselves is no different than working to receive his forgiveness. I do not find any evidence of the need to forgive ourselves in the Bible. I am certain the Lord was pointing out my pride. He was saying, "Who do you think you are? I have forgiven you; it is I who forgives." I was adding other requirements out of my own pride, when all I needed to do was to accept his forgiveness, plain and simple. This sin loomed so large in my life that I felt surely I must be required to do more than that. Mother Teresa knew we can do little, especially in a situation so big. I think she would have said, "It is too big and you are too little. Give it to God."

Now I can see how the radical feminist literature with which I was once enthralled is so contradictory. How can such intellectuals profess that women are more caring than men, yet simultaneously advocate vociferously for abortion? One feminist scholar even refers to the fetus as "an information speck—a set of controlling instructions for a future human being."[2] Language shapes our attitudes and actions. The postmodernist idea that language can construct reality often belies and obscures the very real spiritual and natural impact of words on our choices, our consequences and ultimately our lives and the lives of everyone around us. It is not so much that we construct reality with our words but that we construct what we want to be reality.

The language of God is very different; it works powerfully to keep us walking in the truth. It is both simple enough to guide a child and deep enough to occupy brilliant theologians for a lifetime. That is why so much emphasis is put on Christians' staying saturated in the Word, which is living, active and able to pierce soul and spirit and discern the thoughts and intentions of the heart.[3] At the end of my first year as a Christian, while at a retreat, Abbot Andrew assigned some Scriptures to read before morning. Being tired that evening, I decided to copy them in my notes so that I might review them in the morning. As I wrote, I realized that though I had read the Bible several times by then and listened to it on tape as I walked each day, I had never really seen in these verses what I could see as I wrote them. For the next eight months, I worked some each day to copy by hand the Psalms, Proverbs and New Testament. As I did, I knew my mind was being healed and my understanding of both Christian and secular principles was growing clearer.

I realized one day at Mother Teresa's that in the Bible, pregnancy is not a medical condition, nor is the fetus ever given such an abstract label. In fact, God often named a child at conception or even generations before: "you shall call his name" Mothers are described as being "with child." Mary and Elizabeth meet when they are both "with child." John the Baptist, only six months in the womb of Elizabeth, leapt in recognition of the just-conceived Jesus. These texts have always provided evidence that infants are human beings and that before birth they are aware of facts that perhaps even adults are not.

As a radical feminist, I criticized the abstraction of language about women's bodies, but not in this case. Here the abstraction helped to mask the reality and gave me the freedom to do what I wanted, and what I wanted was not to be bothered. I believe that the abstract medical terminology surrounding "pregnancy" is one of the reasons women like me could see abortions in such a disconnected way, and subsequently why it was so easy to choose abortion. After all, it's treated as a medical condition to be alleviated.

A second reason why the choice for abortion came as easily as it did is that the precious little "counseling" I was offered as a single woman in the doctor's office was in favor of abortion. I was quickly referred to an abortion clinic. Once there, I was told to report to another address, as though it was a secret, and given a false name to use when I arrived. The whole event was cloaked in darkness and deception, which was a spiritual sign I could not or would not read at the time. Many have told me they had the same experience.

One would think that as radical feminists we would support women being treated as intelligent human beings who should be given multiple options with as much information as possible (including the health and psychological risks). These same radical feminist doctrines champion both the idea that women are more caring and relational, and that abortion is a human right—simply one of many choices used to existentially construct a life.

Sadly, the few radical "pro-life" people who say they believe in the sanctity of life and yet are willing to kill doctors and clinic workers are just as alienated from the truth as the radical abortionists. Both contribute to a culture of death.

Abortion was a subject on which Mother Teresa was profusely criticized. I never quite understood why anyone would expect her to think differently, given what she believed and did with her life. When Mother spoke about the tragedy of abortion at a White House breakfast, many were visibly disturbed. Afterward President Clinton commented that it was difficult to argue with a life so well lived: "You have truly lived by what you say."[4] Mother Teresa always worked to combat abortion with adoption. When I was in India, the Missionaries did not adopt many children to the United States because of too many divorces. Mother would say, "A child needs a mother and a father."

Mother was particularly disturbed that wealthy countries aborted so many children:

> In my opinion, if abortion is permitted in wealthy countries that have all the means that money can buy, those countries are the poorest among the poor. . . . It is a noteworthy thing that God should have chosen an unborn baby to give witness to him before the birth of Jesus, but it is sad to think of all the infants that are unborn today through the choice of their parents. . . . Abortion is the greatest destroyer of peace, because we are able to destroy the life that is given by God. If a mother can become the murderer of her children, what can we say about other kinds of murders and wars in the world? Abortion is the source of the evils in the world.[5]

God used the love of Mother and the Missionaries, and my experiences with Babloo, to heal wounds that I still have no words to describe.

24

Give Until It Hurts

FLYING FROM DELHI TO CALCUTTA, I had met a woman
and three men who comprised the front crew for a major event. A
Christian group in the United States had collected an entire plane-
load of drugs and supplies from American and European compa-
nies for distribution to hospitals and clinics, including Mother Teresa's. Federal Express volunteered to fly the supplies to Calcutta.
Being Americans, we began to talk with one another. I noted that
one member of the crew was particularly aloof, maybe even a bit
arrogant. The next week or so, well situated in my volunteer role,
I had forgotten about the whole event when all of a sudden hoards
of visitors deluged the Mother House one morning at Mass. They
filled the chapel and filmed some of the Mass. A great deal of fan-
fare accompanied the group. Mother Teresa and the Missionaries
were very gracious.

I went on to Shishu where a scurry of activity was under way.
The children were dressed in their Sunday clothes though it was

midweek, and the babies wore disposable diapers in anticipation of people holding them. Soon the cameras and visitors showed up also, with a sister leading them on a tour. I saw again the man who had been quite aloof a week before. Now he hugged me, his confidence obviously shaken by the destitution of Calcutta, the work of the Missionaries and the work of other missionaries he had encountered. For two days, strangers poured in and out taking pictures. The Missionaries were gracious, but it was clear that the attention was taking its toll. Mother Teresa had broken her collarbone a few days before. She looked exhausted and dark circles ringed her eyes.

Suddenly I understood what Christ meant when he said, "But when you give to the needy, do not let your left hand know what your right hand is doing, so that your giving may be in secret. And your Father who sees in secret will reward you."[1] How difficult it is to give in secret. The famous twelfth-century rabbi and philosopher Moses Maimonides developed eight levels of charity. One of the highest levels was to give to the poor without knowing them or letting them know you.[2]

Reports circulated in the newspaper about this particular event. Some claimed that certain of the medicines were out of date. Donors had also sent clothes completely unsuited for Calcutta. No complaints arose from the Missionaries. For days afterward while the children napped, they quietly sorted out the winter clothes to send elsewhere in the world. Some of the clothes had obviously been preciously hand sewn, knitted and crocheted. I imagined women in Kansas lovingly stitching clothes and blankets for little children they would never see. This was not lost on the Missionaries who marveled at the careful handiwork, treasuring it as a sign of God's grace. Nothing would be wasted here.

I was reminded that one of Hitchens's complaints in his critical book was that the Missionaries used cotton, cloth diapers instead of the disposable ones they had been sent. The Missionaries only used donated disposables when other people, such as these well-dressed guests from the United States, were going to hold the children, or when taking the children to the doctor or hospitals. Could Hitchens have visited Calcutta, no matter how briefly, and missed noticing the sanitation problems? Imagine in a place with little toilet paper and troublesome sewers trying to dispose of large quantities of disposable diapers.

Privileged people can be quite impractical in places where they do not know the land or the people. Money is usually the best gift. That way those who do know the needs can buy what is most appropriate. I am certain Mother was right—God is not terribly impressed when we simply give away our discards. Recycling is good, but it is not the same as true giving. Mother always said it was best for people to give until it hurt them, for then it was a real sacrifice to God. She said the rich often wanted to share in the hardship of the poor, but only a little bit. The problem was that they did not give until it hurt. A colleague of mine who grew up poor once told me that he feels sorry for people like me who have not been poor because we have so much more to give up. This reminds me of the rich man who wanted to follow Jesus but could not bear to part with his many possessions. Mother called this the poverty of the rich.

Mother told many stories about the generosity of the poor. One of my favorites was about Mother and another sister who delivered a big pot of rice to a Hindu family when they heard that the family had not eaten in days. The mother of eight immediately separated the food into two pots and took one to her Muslim neighbor. When she returned, Mother asked where she had gone. The woman said, "To my neighbors. They are hungry also." Mother said, "I was not surprised that she gave, because poor people are really very generous. But I was surprised that she knew they were hungry. As a rule, when we are suffering, we are so focused on ourselves we have no time for others."[3] Mother Teresa knew that sacrifice—to be real—must cost; we must empty ourselves of something we would rather keep. She said to a group of volunteers, "God takes care of His poor people through us. . . . Remain as 'empty' as possible, so that God can fill you."[4]

25

Revolutionaries for Love

FROM THE BEGINNING, Mother's former students began to join her.

> They wanted to give everything to God, right away. With what joy they put away their colorful saris in order to put on our poor cotton one. They came because they knew it would be hard. When a young woman of high caste comes and puts herself at the service of the poor, she is the protagonist of a revolution. It is the greatest and most difficult revolution— the revolution of love.[1]

After about six weeks, it was becoming clear to me how and why Mother Teresa saw her work as religious work and not as social work. She saw social work as good and helpful. She saw religious work as redemptive because God can do more through human beings than human beings can do on their own. Yet to run this revolution for love, she knew they would have to suffer. Malcolm Muggeridge captures Mother Teresa's words:

Without suffering, our work would just be social work, very good and helpful, but it would not be the work of Jesus Christ, not part of the Redemption. Jesus wanted to help by sharing our life, our loneliness, our agony, our death. Only by being one with us has he redeemed us. We are allowed to do the same; all the desolation of the poor people, not only their material poverty, but their spiritual destitution, must be redeemed, and we must share it, for only by being one with them can we redeem them, that is, by bringing God into their lives and bringing them to God.[2]

Muggeridge asked Mother in an interview if she ever felt a danger that people might mistake the means for the end and believe that serving people was the end in itself. She replied,

There is always the danger that we may . . . do the work for the sake of the work. It is a danger if we forget to whom we are doing it. Our works are only an expression of our love for Christ . . . since we have to express that love in action, naturally then the poorest of the poor are the means of expressing our love for God.[3]

She came to believe in her later years that the most devastating disease of humanity was not illness, hunger or poverty, but loneliness and the sense of being unloved that she encountered in people all over the world. The Missionaries serve some simply by visiting them regularly.

I think one of Mother's favorite stories was about an elderly man in Australia who lived in appalling conditions. The sisters asked if they could please clean his house. He argued that he was fine, but they urged him anyway, saying he would be better off with a clean house. He agreed, and as they cleaned, they discovered a beautiful lamp covered with dirt. They inquired if he ever used it. He told them that no one ever came to his house, so why would he need to light the lamp? They said, "If we come to see you, would you light the lamp?" He agreed, and they began to visit him regularly. He lived another two years and kept his house clean. He sent Mother a message, "Tell my friend that the light that she lit in my life is still shining."[4]

Studs Terkel, in his study of work in America, said that many people are unhappy in their jobs because, as he quoted an interviewee, "Most of us have jobs that are too small for our spirits."[5] Mother Teresa showed me that no job is too small, but my spirit may be. She showed me that it is less about the actual work and more about the attitudes and the spirit in which we do it. Our call is to work to the best of our ability and to do it with and for God. The faithfulness with which we perform a current job builds the character needed for the next one. Martin Luther King Jr. said, "If it falls your lot to be a street sweeper, go on out and sweep streets like Michelangelo painted pictures. . . . Sweep streets so well that all the hosts of heaven and earth will have to pause and say, 'Here lived a great street sweeper who swept his job well.'"[6]

Mother said, "Vocation means Jesus has called us by name."[7] In her mind, all humans have one vocation—to belong to God. But within that lie many different callings: business entrepreneurs, political leaders, mothers, mechanics, teachers, lawyers, salespersons, nurses, police, gardeners, artists, waiters. The list is endless.

I have met many who look for something difficult to do for God and other people. In the modern world, our lives with God can become increasingly separate from our lives at work. Yet today more young adults are dedicating themselves to working and living among the poor with Christ. One book calls these young Christians "the new friars."[8] I wonder how much Mother's life contributed to the explosion of ministries to the poor.

I sometimes imagine what could be done if a significant number of young Christians decided to make the education of inner-city youth their focus. What if they went two-by-two and four-by-four into urban schools, devoting themselves to prayer and hard work, and committed their sufferings to building their own character as well as the students'?

There are an infinite number of possible revolutions for love and many potential protagonists. I do not want to suggest naively that we easily can be like the Missionaries, and I am certain Mother Teresa would not recommend that we emulate them exactly. I believe they are in a class unto themselves. Nevertheless, for every possible revolution of love, whether in government, schools, hospitals, homes, or the streets, I believe there are ways we would need to imitate the Missionaries in order to be effective.

First, they have committed their lives to God, have a strong relationship with Christ, and hear from and move in his Holy Spirit. They have a leader with a distinct call and others who corroborate the same call. They have found a way to live in community with other believers and learned to work side-by-side. They vigorously keep themselves from worldliness, yet work deeply in the troubled heart of the world. They love those with whom they work both inside and outside the community, not soulishly, not expecting any return. They pray, worship and study unceasingly. They constantly build their minds and character to become more like Jesus and let his power, love and wisdom work through them to build up their part of the body of Christ.

I believe any successful revolutionary for love will also suffer, as did Mother and as do the Missionaries. Our suffering may only be in terms of the natural pain of separation from others who misunderstand or don't approve of the choice to decline being "of the world." Yet, it can go so far as imprisonment and death. In the world, an average of 171,000 Christians are martyred each year.[9] For every measure of suffering that does not lead to martyrdom, there is extraordinary grace to overcome. Perhaps more important, on the other side of suffering rightly, there is always an advance in character—a growth in holiness. Living in community or having a close group of like-minded friends who are prayerful and godly is essential in helping us stay the course, discern the trials, persevere and grow in holiness. Mother said, "Suffering in itself is nothing, but suffering shared with the passion of Christ is a wonderful gift . . . because suffering was how he paid for sin."[10]

26

Mother Teresa
and the Body of Christ

B<small>Y THE TIME</small> I <small>ARRIVED AT</small> M<small>OTHER</small> T<small>ERESA'S</small>, I had experienced many parts of Christ's body. I was learning from Protestants, Catholics and Orthodox, from monks and mothers, from young and old, rich and poor. Soon after my conversion, my colleague, friend and mentor, John Rivera, gave me two conference brochures from opposite ends of the Christian spectrum—an evangelical conference and a retreat at a charismatic monastery. I attended both.

At Bill Gothard's conference, I heard Scripture explained in terms of basic life principles. This lit an unquenchable fire in my heart to study the Bible. By contrast, Pecos Monastery used Scripture for inner healing. The priests, sisters and monks there set me to discovering the person of Jesus and who I really was in the context of Scripture. Now at Mother Teresa's, I was rapidly developing a sense that the divisions in Christ's body between denominations,

race, class, nationality and giftings must be one of the most grievous things to God. It seemed to me that each denomination did a
good job of understanding and manifesting particular aspects of
Christ, but was weaker in others. Mother Teresa was called into
the part of the body of Christ called Catholicism.

The Missionaries of Charity are unique in many ways, but one
of the most profound is that Jesus called Mother to establish an
order that would be Indian, not European. Before the Missionaries
were established, her Bishop asked her whether or not the work
could be accomplished through an existing congregation.

> No. First, because they are European. When our Indian
> girls enter these orders—they are made to live their life—
> eat, sleep, dress like them. In a word, as people say—they
> become Mems [European women]. They have no chance of
> feeling the Holy Poverty. Second—as much as those Sisters
> try to adapt themselves to the country, they remain foreign-
> ers for the people—and then there are their rules—which
> do not allow them so to say, be one of the people. They have
> their big schools and hospitals—in all these the souls have
> to come to them or be brought to them. While the Missionar-
> ies of Charity will go in search, live their days in the slums
> and streets. Close to the people's heart—they would do the
> works of Christ in their very homes—in the dirty and dark
> holes of the street beggars. As Our Lord himself says, "There
> are plenty of nuns to look after the rich and able to do peo-
> ple—but for My very poor, there are absolutely none. For
> them I long—them I love." He also asks for Indian Nuns—
> dressed in Indian clothes—leading the Indian life.[1]

Today Mother Teresa's Missionaries around the world form a
multiracial, multinational and multiclass community from every
tribe and tongue and people and nation.[2] Paul writes in several of

his letters that in the body of Christ there is no male or female, Jew or Greek, slave or free.[3]

God ordains one way for all people to come together, and that is to gather under the headship of Christ. Christians who are Catholic, Orthodox, Protestant, Pentecostal and evangelical, gentile and Jewish, rich and poor, of all tribes, races, cultures, languages and nationalities—all make up the body of Christ. People from each of these divisions have taught me things about God. Through them, I see the wholeness and beauty of the body of Christ. Despite denominational differences, those who helped me were all "orthodox" believers. They shared several things in common: a strong belief in the Bible as the Word of God, a personal relationship with Christ as Lord, continuous confession of their sins, a deep desire to grow in things of God, knowledge that God has a purpose for their life and a burning desire to fulfill that purpose.

Those who have taught me most often have not been of my race or culture, but are friends who walk in the Spirit, love God with an intensity that I long for and are unrelenting in their pursuit of truth. They are willing to give up whatever is required in order to mature spiritually. They constantly hunger and thirst for righteousness, and the most important thing to each of them, like to Mother Teresa, is to hear and obey God in order to fulfill their destiny. Their feelings and rationalizations do not dictate their lives, just as Mother's feelings of brokenness did not deter her work or life with Christ. Because of the way God has raised me to know and love so many parts of his body, it is difficult for me to frame myself within the usual denominational categories. I often find myself explaining one part of the body to another.

The body of Christ is the mystical body made up of all believers in Jesus Christ; we are all parts of a larger living organism, empowered by the Holy Spirit. We have the potential to come together, live in peace and work as one because none of us is the head. Christ is the head. When he truly leads us, all our destinies and purposes work together to bless others and increase his peace on earth. Though we are far from our potential, the more Christlike we become, the more we are able to work together. Yet Christianity is not a utopian idea, we are to remain aware of our weaknesses and constantly lift them to God who can work powerfully through weaknesses. Indeed Paul tells us that God works best in our weakness.[4] Power is a central part of all radical philosophy and ideology in the academy, but in Christianity power belongs ultimately to God alone.

Submitting to Christ's headship includes obeying the principles and precepts with which God designed the universe. Just as the designer of a machine writes a manual that explains how optimally to use it, God also designed the universe to operate along certain principles. When we follow these, we also "work optimally." God's principles of health and psychology are just as sure and active as his law of gravity. If forgiveness is a true principle around which human beings are designed to operate, then breaking that principle through unforgiveness will have a similar effect as defying gravity by jumping off a building. It may take us longer to die, but unforgiveness begins immediately to wreak its destructive effects in our minds and bodies.

Mother knew that she and her sisters would not have the strength to fulfill their call without a deep and personal relationship with Christ. In a letter to the sisters on protecting this relationship, she wrote:

> Be careful of all that can block that personal contact with the living Jesus. The devil may try to use the hurts of life, and sometimes our own mistakes to make you feel it is impossible that Jesus really loves you, is really cleaving to you.

This is a danger for all of us. And so sad, because it is completely the opposite of what Jesus is really wanting, waiting to tell you. Not only that He loves you, but even more—He longs for you. He misses you when you don't come close. He thirsts for you. He loves you always, even when you don't feel worthy. When not accepted by others, even by yourself sometimes—he is the one who always accepts you. My children, you don't have to be different for Jesus to love you. Only believe—you are precious to Him. Bring all your suffering to His feet—only open your heart to be loved by Him as you are. He will do the rest.[5]

All Christians in all denominations are called to develop and protect this relationship with Christ, as well as to discover and answer their call, no matter whether they do it as clumsily as I or as superbly as Mother Teresa. Our callings are so diverse as to be innumerable—mother, soldier, farm worker, executive, teacher, president. With Christ abiding in us, our growth is assured because we are filled with God's grace. A Christian can never stay the same; we are either growing forward or falling backward in our spiritual lives.

The Catholic church has given and continues to give great gifts to the body of Christ and to the world, such as preserving the holiness and reverence for the Eucharist; championing issues of justice, the sanctity of life and marriage; and preserving the beauty of the liturgy and the scriptural soundness of liturgical music. Catholicism is not perfect because people are not perfect. Are all its doctrines biblical? Of course not, because like every other denomination, it relies on tradition and the writings of imperfect humans and has tendencies to over- or under-emphasize particular Scriptures in its doctrines. Since different groups have different revelations and gifts, we all function better working together, just like the parts of a body working in coordination to function best.

I believe it is because of the power of belonging to the body of Christ that Christians over the centuries have led almost every successful campaign for human freedom ranging from antislavery to women's suffrage and child protection. Even Gandhi, a Hindu, regarded Christ as a model. He said in his autobiography that he disliked the Old Testament but "the Sermon on the Mount went straight to my heart."[6] Racial reconciliation services have become a normal part of the orthodox Christian landscape.

Martin Luther King Jr. captured the essence of a principle on which the body of Christ functions when he said, "For some strange reason I can never be what I ought to be until you are what you ought to be. And you can never be what you ought to be until I am what I ought to be. That is the way God's universe is made."[7] Two of the principles for becoming one body are that those who seem least important are most important, and that when one part of the body hurts, all are hurt.[8] Mother believed she was the perfect example of another principle of the body of Christ—that God chooses those who look the weakest to confound the strong and those who look foolish to confound the wise.

The body of Christ is being built in the world as never before. Mother Teresa's life was one of the most brilliant signs of it. It is everywhere, all over the earth, emerging rapidly in Africa, South America and Asia. Evidences of renewal are present even in Europe and the United States. Reconciliation efforts are healing long-standing divisions in Christ's body. Orthodoxy is still on the increase.[9] Those in the popular media who are not orthodox believers tend to poorly interpret Christianity and instead focus on specific personalities that often do not represent the dominant moves of Christianity in the world today.

The body of Christ is you and I, believers in Christ all over the planet, in secular workplaces, schools and hospitals, universities and businesses, governments and shopping malls, in construction and the entertainment industry, on farms and in cities, and in our churches and homes. It is a magnificent thing to be a molecule in the body of Christ. No matter where we live in the world, we are instantly joined to a larger body. I have visited believers in other countries, and though we could hardly say a word to one another, we communicated through our eyes. Sometimes the power of this connection to Christ was so strong that we simply looked at one another and wept. We knew that we loved the same God and that through him we were uniquely connected in relationship. This can happen between any two orthodox believers no matter what their denomination, country, economic status or race.

27

The Uniqueness of Christ

⋙⋘

MOTHER TERESA AND THE MISSIONARIES primarily
served Muslims, lower caste Hindus, or those without a religion.
She never denigrated other religions. She firmly believed that
every person is a child of God, and she wanted to bring Christ to
everyone. She was not naive; she did not believe that all religions
are essentially the same, or will lead to the same place, or that
anyone can create a religion to unify them.

Similarly, the Dalai Lama said in a public lecture in Pasadena, California, that Christ and Buddha will not take you
to the same place. A Buddhist, for example, ultimately seeks
nirvana, a state of peace beyond suffering. The Buddha's key
question was how to avoid suffering, and his answer was to
transcend desire. Buddhists reach this state of enlightenment
by giving up desires and becoming one with nature, with all
sentient beings, through their own efforts. In this way, a Buddhist adds to the peace of the world.

For Mother Teresa, suffering is part of life in a broken universe. Allowing God to purify our desires and use our sufferings is essential to knowing and fulfilling our life's purpose. God wants to give us the desires of our hearts, not for us to deny them.[1]

A Christian's first desire is to acknowledge and submit to God, receive forgiveness for sins, and deepen in relationship with him. The Holy Spirit then works to purify and clarify our desires, which form the basis of the purpose and meaning of our lives. The closer we come to Christ, the more united our desires become with God's and the more we are empowered to fulfill our purpose. Suffering is part of this process. Overcoming suffering in right ways actually helps build the character we need to fulfill our calling. This is accomplished not solely or even primarily because of our valiant efforts and great skill. Suffering is an essential part of being Christian. Christians must be willing to suffer, even to die for others—never to die killing those who refuse Christ, but possibly to die while serving others. To Mother Teresa suffering was an opportunity to unite ourselves to Christ, to make reparation and to become more holy.

Christ was not a human philosopher crafting erudite questions and answers throughout his life. He came from God as the incarnate Word, to be the answer. He showed us the way to live the kingdom of God on earth. Thus Christianity is not a human philosophy. Jesus wrote no books, directed no wars and led no nations. He never answered a human question with yes or no; he always had a better way. Jesus claimed he was the Son of God. This statement eventually led to his crucifixion. If he is not the Son of God, he lied, and thus he cannot be merely a good person. A good person would not lie about something so monumental. So he forced us to choose; there is no in-between. The historical evidence we have suggests that he was perfect and the most powerful person to have ever lived.

Unlike other religions, Christianity is not the possession of a particular people group, culture, region of the world or socioeconomic group. Christ commanded his disciples to "go into all the world and proclaim the gospel to the whole creation."[2] This is one of the commands most criticized by non-Christians, yet every person tries to convince others of their worldview. In other words, most people evangelize. I certainly did in my former days. I have often wondered what it is about Christ that made this evangelization seem so much more extreme. Is the truth that much harder to accept than a lie?

Missionaries have written books illuminating the errors of transmitting characteristics of one culture to another when sharing the gospel.[3] That was what Mother Teresa did not want to do with her order; she wanted Indian girls to be able to serve Christ in the context of their culture and not have to act like Europeans. Yet the notion that Christianity transforms culture is also true; Christ desires that cultures change. Unhealthy things exist in every culture. Believers are called to be in the world, but not of the world. Theologian Lesslie Newbigin writes, "There can never be a culture-free gospel. Yet the gospel . . . calls into question all cultures including the one in which it was originally embodied."[4]

Though the gospel challenges all cultures, the variety of cultures also expresses God's diversity. Each has gifts to contribute to the world. Like different denominations, cultures highlight or reveal unique aspects of the gospel. However, unlike what popular Western culture promotes, not all diversity is desirable. Not every cell in a body is healthy or helpful; some are diseased. We must learn to discern based on principles and precepts of God. All races, all classes, all cultures and all nations contain people and traditions that are healthy and unhealthy, good and evil, life-giving and life-destroying. Each of us contains both the healthy and unhealthy, as well.

While Christianity is often classified as a Western religion, it neither began in the West nor is it confined to the West; it has from its beginning been for all people. While early Christian communities existed in India, Ethiopia and Egypt, Europe was the first to benefit from incorporating Judeo-Christian[5] principles into the foundational principles of institutions and in the laws of nations. Currently, approximately one-third of the world confesses Christ. Christians from Africa, South America and Asia are now also sending missionaries to other nations and to the West to help it recover its lost love.[6] Reports abound of Christ performing miracles, signs and wonders all over the world, but not only does the West witness fewer miracles, we believe less.[7]

To Mother, Jesus was everything, the reason for her life and power behind her work. I imagine of all the words Jesus spoke to her she must have held these most dearly: "My little spouse, My own little one."[8]

28

Leaving Calcutta

W HEN I LEFT THE MISSIONARIES IN CALCUTTA, I flew
to Jerusalem to meet my friend Geralyn, a Benedictine sister. She
was completing studies of Judaic prayer and the Hebrew prophets.
I joined her during the last week of her courses, and we toured
some of the sites significant to Christ's life in Jerusalem. We
stayed at a Franciscan monastery built on the site of John the Baptist's birth. I arrived with a stomach virus that had prohibited me
from eating for three days. As I contracted the virus, Babloo was
set free from his. The first night in Jerusalem, I had a dream that I
was holding baby Babloo. He looked up at me and in a man's voice
said, "God said I could give you anything you want; what do you
want?" In the dream I said, "The Spirit of God." He closed his eyes
and nodded yes and I awoke. I learned after I returned that Babloo
went home to be with his family two days after I left Calcutta.

While the virus stayed with me a few more days, I found I
was strong in spirit from my time with the Missionaries. Even

though I had not eaten for days, I was able to walk a few miles to another monastery where John the Baptist supposedly lived for a while. From there, we traveled with Geralyn's group (mostly priests) on a tour of other Biblical sites in Turkey and Greece. Then she and I went on to Italy and France to see other Christian religious work.

We stopped at various monasteries and visited the school of Sofia Cavaletti, a woman who spent her life elaborating on the Christian spiritual development of children. This was work begun by Maria Montessori.[1] At Cavaletti's school in Rome we saw the spiritual education of children age three to twelve.

Also in Rome, Geralyn and I walked to the convent of the sisters of St. Frances of Rome, a saint who had tended the poor during the Middle Ages, much like Mother Teresa. We arrived at their door on Pentecost Sunday. Geralyn knew they were cloistered and never admitted guests, but she had prayed for many months that we would be admitted. On our way to the convent, Geralyn informed me for the first time that they were cloistered and had never admitted anyone from outside their monastery, but then she nonchalantly added, "The Holy Spirit told me you would get us in." As a new and naive Christian that seemed completely out of the realm of possibility, and I began to tell Geralyn this; she was unfazed. We continued walking and I got out my "How to Speak Italian" card and tried to think of what I would say, knowing it would have to be mostly Spanish, if even that.

We approached the daunting doors that had glass fortified by iron bars, and when I rang the doorbell, we could see a nun approach a phone on the other side of a second set of doors. She answered, and I began as best I could to say we were from the United States and loved Francis of Rome, and could we please visit. The nun told me in no uncertain terms that it would be "impossible" (a word remarkably similar in all three languages). I acted as though I did not understand the word and began to ask: "Could we come back in an hour, later in the afternoon, tomorrow?" She said impossible again, hung up and went back to where she had come from. I looked at Geralyn who had tears gathering at the bottom of her eyes. She said, "The Holy Spirit told me."

Seeing her about to cry, I became emboldened and repeated, pretty much, the same sequence, adding that we had a book to give them. The nun went away again, and then I rang again. We noticed that she came back this time with a key and began to unlock both doors. Once we were inside, she pointed up a long staircase and instructed us, with considerable exasperation, to go to "La Madre." Once upstairs, the Mother of the order called another nun, who happened to have just arrived from New York, to translate for our tour. We were able to give the convent a book about St. Francis written by one of Geralyn's colleagues who had received the inspiration in a dream.[2] Geralyn was ecstatic.

That night in a small restaurant, we marveled at all the gifts the sisters had given us—pictures of mural paintings of St. Francis's life that we had seen inside the convent and even a bit of salve made from Francis of Rome's formula. A young priest dining with his parents walked over and gave us each a rosary blessed by the Pope that very day; he said it was because he could see in our faces that we loved God.

Another evening in Rome, while waiting to go to a restaurant that was closed, we found a church still open and entered. As I sat in a front pew, I began to feel drawn to a beautiful icon of Christ on a stand in the front. In the icon of a rich, yellow-gold color, Jesus was holding an open Bible with one hand and making a gesture of blessing with the other. In my spirit, I heard three times distinctly, "Teach my people." I asked a couple of English-speaking priests also visiting the church if they knew the name of the icon. One told me it was called "Christ the Teacher"!

At one of the French monasteries, we met a woman who invited me to spend the week at her Paris flat and even took me to her country home. We were both Benedictine oblates to related monasteries. This was a tremendous blessing, and it afforded me the opportunity to locate and spend a day at the original L'Arche community begun by Jean Vanier in France. A L'Arche community is where people with disabilities and some without—though everyone there acknowledges their brokenness—live, pray and work together.[3] Mother Teresa and Jean Vanier met one another many times.

Suddenly I began to understand at a deeper level why I had prayed that God would allow the trip only if it was his will.[4] The entire return journey was filled with supernatural grace. Everywhere we were offered unusual opportunities, and strangers would walk up and bless us in different ways. We both felt that within the gifts were messages which we would continue to unravel for years.

At night, I would lie awake and reflect on the various stories of miracles among the Missionaries, the healing of Babloo, his love for the picture of Jesus, the bottle nipple that arrived just in time, the Indian money, the special help to the Delhi plane, the entry into the cloistered monastery, the voice from the icon . . . So many experiences rolled around in me with nowhere to put them. I hardly had any categories that could accommodate my experiences. My old categories of coincidence and serendipity crumbled under the weight of new experiences and understandings.

The Lord was resurrecting something that had long laid dormant in me, and I was beginning to come more alive. I felt like a child allowed into my Father's study for the first time to experience certain secrets. I was seeing things I had never noticed before. Like a child, I was pointing to them and waiting for him to give me the word.

29

Finding Calcutta

W<small>HEN</small> I <small>RETURNED TO THE</small> U<small>NITED</small> S<small>TATES</small> in June, I
finished the last two months of my sabbatical with family and
friends in Texas. In late August, I returned to teaching at the university where I had taught before.

I am not a person who cries often or easily. However, for the first
couple of months of the term, I would go into my office to prepare
for class from the readings I had given the graduate students, the
books on my shelves and articles in my files. There I would burst
into tears without a preceding emotion. I could not understand
this strange phenomenon. It was not the usual reentry problem as
I had been in the States for about two months by then. I harbored
no notion that I belonged in Calcutta or was to stop what I was doing to work directly with the poor. They were uncommon tears. I
prayed for weeks that God would reveal their origin and purpose,
but the answer was not forthcoming. The weeping continued un-
abated, though it always stopped in time for class.

Only recently did someone help me find Symeon, the New Theologian from the tenth century, who developed quite a theology about tears.[1] He believed that such tears were a gift of the Holy Spirit and that part of their purpose was to soften a hardened heart and lead a person to repentance, purification and further contemplation. Certainly, my tears were doing all those things, but I did not understand them or enjoy them. I am a "thinking type" on personality tests, and "thinking types" don't like to cry in the first place. But if we must cry, surely we should at least intellectually understand why. God obviously did not share my opinion for a couple of months.

Then one day in October, I spoke at a breakfast for women school administrators at their annual conference. They had invited me to share about my time with Mother Teresa. I told them stories not unlike the ones in this book. During the question-and-answer session, a woman asked if it had been difficult coming back from Mother Teresa's community. I was immediately overwhelmed with the same tears in front of what was well over one hundred professional women. As I stood there trying to regain my composure, I suddenly received the answer to my prayer.

Seeing as it was such a relief to me and because she had asked, I blurted out my newfound answer to prayer without thinking about the secular setting. I told them, yes, I had obviously had some trouble. A nervous laughter of relief rippled through the crowd. Then I continued to share that I had been a Christian for three years, and I had met many people including Mother Teresa who showed me the truth and power of Christianity. However, as I prepared to teach, I now realized that the only worldview I was leaving out of my classes was the Christian worldview. I said that if anything in Christianity was true, I was withholding it from my graduate students. I felt like a liar. At that, other women in the audience began to cry and the meeting ended.

I had found my Calcutta.

30

My Thoughts Are
Not Your Thoughts

For my thoughts are not your thoughts,
Neither are your ways my ways, declares the LORD.
For as the heavens are higher than the earth,
So are my ways higher than your ways
And my thoughts than your thoughts.

ISAIAH 55:8-9

≽⋐

THE REVELATION OF MY CALCUTTA began as a deep intellectual and personal crisis. In the three years prior to Calcutta, I
had struggled to understand my newfound faith and its meaning.
I had read and reread the Bible and acquainted myself with many
parts of the body of Christ. For me these three years had caused
my life to be at once interrupted and enhanced. (Mother Teresa
also had a three-year period from 1928-1931 when she had gone
through spiritual formation under the direction of the Sisters of
Loreto.) As I began to seek to understand biblical Christianity, I

began to realize that the more completely one lived it, the more distanced one felt from the culture.

I had first begun to realize how different Christianity was in the way my colleague John Rivera thought, spoke and lived out his calling. Though we had worked together on various projects for years, for a long while I did not know he was a Christian. I could hardly understand the counsel he would give me—the way he thought about issues of education, culture, business, policy and life—yet his wisdom always rang so true. His life had been filled with trials, yet there was no sign of the usual "oppressed" anger in him. Instead a deep peace that was disconcerting to me constantly accompanied him. When I said to him one day in the summer of 1995 that I would like to work with Mother Teresa, he immediately replied, "Go and go soon." I wrote the Missionaries shortly afterward.

Now I had had the experience of living day in and day out near Mother Teresa. Neither her life nor John Rivera's life made much sense to me compared to what I had been taught and the way I had always lived my life. Even when compared to other Christians I had met, their lives were more extreme in terms of purpose, humility, clarity and purity. They seemed like characters from the Bible transplanted in the twentieth century. I began to wonder how I would have to change to be even half as clear and faithful to my calling as they were to theirs.

Often people teach that to know our calling, we must know our spiritual gifts, desires, opportunities and special skills. Clearly, these are all useful. However, it is perhaps even more the case that our crises and grievings reveal our call. Moreover, answering our call is not always exhilarating. Throughout the Bible, people realized and fulfilled their special destinies through tribulations and sufferings, like Mother Teresa. The injustices in the education of the poor already concerned me; now I grieved over the narrowness of the worldviews in the university and my complicity in promoting it.

By the time I got to Mother Teresa's, I had been given all the grace I needed to overcome my most egregious and obvious sinful behaviors. But suddenly I had to face the fact that what I was teaching, I no longer believed; and that what I now believed, I was neither teaching nor living—an ever-present challenge. Still I knew, at least for now, that I was called to remain in the university where I was at. I knew then as now, that graduate students should be well educated in all of the worldviews. There was only one problem: I was not teaching them all. I was, like most professors, teaching only secular perspectives (though I was throwing in some pantheistic ones as well). I began to realize just how much faith it had taken for me to believe these. Every worldview demands faith in its foundational principles. While our various methods of research answer many questions, a worldview's foundational beliefs are not provable; they also require faith. I had come to have many faiths, regardless of their contradictory natures.

On a plane ride one day, I suddenly came to a startling realization that emerged from seeing the relationship between the first chapters of Genesis, John, Colossians and Hebrews. Genesis 1:1-3 informs us that "in the beginning . . . the Spirit of God was hovering over the face of the waters. And God said, 'Let there be light' and there was light." I saw distinctly the three moving as one—God, his Spirit and his Word. What a miracle that these three always agree! The Gospel of John reveals more about the Word that God spoke, "In the beginning was the Word, and the Word was with God, and the Word was God. He was in the beginning with God. All things were made through him, and without him was not anything made that was made. . . . And the Word became flesh and dwelt among us."[1] Paul tells us in Hebrews that Jesus "is the exact imprint of God's very being,"[2] and in Colossians that "by him all things were created . . . and in him all things hold together."[3] I asked myself, *If these are true, then how could anything I taught not relate to God, the Holy Spirit and Jesus?* Philosopher Dallas Willard puts it more directly: "Jesus is the smartest man who ever lived."[4]

Upon these revelations, my first instinct was to reject all of the secular philosophies and theories I had been teaching. This was a mistake because, from a Christian worldview, while these other theories would contain principles distorted by errors of omission or commission, they would also contain true ones. No theory or philosophy can be entirely false; else, it cannot stand. Evil cannot create; it can only distort and destroy. Jesus called it "sow[ing] weeds among the wheat."[5] The most critical thing then for me was to discern. I needed to (1) identify the foundational principles in what I was teaching, (2) learn to discern the true from false ones and (3) try to identify any true principles that are absent. Because I (and most of us, even in Christian universities) have been educated in doctoral programs solely from the secular worldviews in our fields, these are difficult things to do. To my delight, I soon discovered there are excellent scholars struggling to do this in their own fields, and there are organizations that provide temporary meeting places for us to come together.[6]

I literally needed to apply Paul's admonition: "Present your bodies as a living sacrifice, holy and acceptable to God, which is your spiritual worship. Do not be conformed to this world, but be transformed by the renewal of your mind, that by testing you may discern what is the will of God, what is good and acceptable and perfect."[7]

I briefly considered moving to a Christian college, but all those prayers and opportunities seemed to be met with a stone wall from God. Besides, how could my moving help broaden the worldviews in the mainline research academy? I realized I was to stay, but where could I start? I was not hired to teach only or even primarily Christian principles. Earlier I had left them out because of my ignorance and rebelliousness; now I was leaving them out largely out of a fear of rejection. Neither reason was intellectually sound. I was limiting the education of all my students when I had the call and the ability to broaden it. After all, the university pledges itself to academic freedom in the pursuit of truth—Veritas—as the Harvard seal proclaims.[8] However, I knew from experience that the Christian worldview was not part of the diversity valued in the academy. Indeed, I myself had dismissed it with great hostility. A graduate recalled some years later that in my radical feminism class I told students they could use any source in their papers except the Bible. I had never considered Mother Teresa as an example for educated women to follow, though she had developed a worldwide, multicultural compassion ministry.

I had once lived like Rahab the harlot, and the university accepted me with open arms. As one colleague put it, "She used to be the party girl." Now I felt like a leper at the country club. I had only one colleague and one friend (who were not Christian) from my pre-Christian days who could bear more than a minute in conversation about my newfound worldview. I probably would not have lasted that long in my earlier years. I remember when people would talk to me about Christ, I would immediately begin to fade out mentally and become uncomfortable emotionally. Thinking I was feeling sorry for them for being so naive and foolish, I would seek to change the topic as soon as possible. However, the truth was that my mind was veiled to the reality they were describing. I could neither bear to hear nor begin to understand what they were saying. It was not so much the vague ideas of God or the Spirit that would upset and confuse me; even though uninformed I could talk about those things. However, the name of Jesus set my spirit on edge; I was of other spirits.

I knew I had to address the crisis by finding a way in the university to teach Christian principles where they offered actual alternatives, in addition to the principles of other worldviews, to broaden the options for my students. At first, I began teaching a class specifically on Christian principles and education in the summers. I chose summers because, if a course does not have enough enrollees in the summer, the university is not obliged to pay me. How could anyone argue with that arrangement? I quickly discovered that there were many strong Christian students in the graduate program, and a number of them were teaching at Christian universities that required them to integrate Christian principles into the subject matter of education and other fields. They had no more idea than I did how to do this, but we were all eager.

The first day of the first summer I offered the class, I had six students enrolled, but I needed seven. On the way to class, I felt the Lord was asking me to teach the course even without pay. I did not mention canceling the class; the six students and I dove into our first daylong Saturday session. After the lunch break, the seventh student came in apologizing for being late and for not having yet registered. Ever since, I have taught the class in the summer, and it has always had enough students. It has changed over the years and is now primarily a course where the graduate students and I study the prevailing contemporary philosophies and theories through a Christian lens, discerning the complementary and contradictory principles. The Petries' video about Mother Teresa helps us begin a discussion on the differences between secular humanism and Christian principles. Other videos introduce the students to different parts of the body of Christ.

Now slowly I began to integrate Christian principles along with all the others I teach. So when we study issues of poverty and justice in education, I laid out the options side by side: principles of developmental psychology, liberal humanism, behaviorism, feminism, Marxism (critical theory), Christianity, and any other worldview they or I know.

I believe that most of the professors who disregard the Christian worldview in their work are not even conscious of the intellectual loss they face by doing so, and most are certainly not as hostile as I was, though some are. Most simply have no idea that Christianity has intellectual, social, psychological, artistic, scientific, ecological and economic principles embedded throughout its worldview and that, in most cases, these principles challenge the ones we currently teach. The Christian worldview is unique, intellectually and spiritually, as well as morally.

To more effectively teach and better understand my calling, I began to study the history of the university and Western philosophy, as well as dominant worldviews and their assumptions.[9] Charles Colson and Nancy Pearcey urge all of us to consider this, "If we are going to make a difference in our world, we must grasp these profoundly contrary views of reality, for they are the root of our cultural crisis."[10] (For readers who would like a sketch of some of my discoveries in these areas, as well as a vision for renewing secular universities and developing new Christian ones, there are two appendixes in the back of the book.)

There are three dominant worldviews in today's university—naturalism, secular humanism and pantheism. Naturalism is the belief that the material of the natural world is all that exists and that no spiritual reality exists behind or beyond the material world—no God. Secular humanism is the belief that human beings have intellectually, socially and morally evolved to the place where we no longer need to invent God. We are capable and responsible for creating a better world without religious trappings. Pantheism is the belief that the divine exists in us and in the natural world as energy. We are one with the divine. Its proponents often declare themselves "spiritual but not religious."

Suffice it to say that, from any of the dominant worldviews in today's university, Mother Teresa's beliefs, the way she lived her life and the power behind her work are completely incomprehensible and offensive. When viewed from these worldviews one must distort who she was. Richard John Neuhaus wrote of her, "In a world captive to wealth and glitter and power, her witness kept alive the rumor that there is a radically different measure of human greatness. And even those whom the world counts as great half suspected that she was right."[11]

Todd Lake described the struggle to understand and accept her Christian worldview in the university:

> I remember Mother Teresa's speech on the steps of Memorial Church at the Class Day exercise [Harvard graduation] in 1982, where she talked of Jesus incessantly—I mean incessantly—and even quoted that verse, John 3:16 (already known to most of us, thanks to signs in the end-zone bleachers). But in a triumph of brilliant editing, Harvard Magazine's account managed to report almost the entire Mother Teresa speech without once hinting that she might even have mentioned Jesus. We all sensed he could be trouble, and we wanted to make sure he never became a live issue.[12]

While working on my doctoral degree at the University of Texas, I frequently passed the main building, the UT Tower, on my way to "the drag." This was where street vendors and New Age practitioners worked side-by-side with hamburger vendors and the psychedelic ice cream shop we frequented when we were high. Etched in stone across the front of that building are the words: "Ye shall know the truth and the truth will set you free." I was completely unaware that these were the words of Jesus. For the most part, we made fun of them. I remember, for example, one group of students that was running for office promised in their campaign pledge to change the words to the "real" truth, which they said was "Money

Talks." They were elected; the truth words survived their tenure.

While these words frequently appear on university buildings, they are not some secular promise that everything students are about to study will lead them to truth. It is also not the full statement, which reads:

> If you abide in my word, you are truly my disciples, and you will know the truth, and the truth will set you free.[13]

When Jesus said these words, some of the Jews listening to him protested, "We are offspring of Abraham and have never been enslaved to anyone. How is it that you say, 'You will become free?'" All the while, Roman armies marched through their streets and occupied the seats of government.

Like them, I thought I was free and good, but all the while my mind was becoming darker, my self looming larger and my character descending into a deep abyss. While I was making up my own truths in graduate school, Mother Teresa was beginning her third decade of living out the Truth on the streets of Calcutta.

Epilogue

Fall More in Love with Jesus Every Day

Bᴇɪɴɢ ɪɴ ᴛʜᴇ ᴘʀᴇsᴇɴᴄᴇ ᴏғ Mother Teresa and the Missionaries was to be in the presence of holiness, and that holiness could express itself in prophetic ways. I do not think Mother had any idea how often she did this. She may not have always felt Jesus' presence, but many of us experienced his presence through her.

One of my last mornings in Calcutta, I was sent back to the Mother House to pick up some materials for one of the sisters at Shishu Bhavan. I was sitting on the bench between the office and chapel on the second floor, waiting for the sister to return with the materials. Mother Teresa emerged from behind the fabric that hung in the doorway. We had seen each other almost every day and occasionally had brief encounters, but she did not know anything about me. Our eyes were level as she stood and I sat on the bench. When she saw me, she began immediately to shake her finger at me. Our eyes locked on one another. She exclaimed with great urgency, "You fall more in love with Jesus every day!" I quickly replied with the only thing I could get out of my mouth, "Yes, Ma'am." This message came straight from her spirit into mine; it had not yet even entered my mind.

That was all she said, and she continued walking. I felt as though every cell in my body had jumped to attention. Her words reverberated through me as if I had been physically hit. The full impact of her command began to sink in as I walked back to Shishu Bhavan.

Mother had no way of knowing that I was a professor, yet through the Holy Spirit, she perceived that my faith tends to stay in my mind. She was warning me to move it to my heart as well. I believe I will continue to struggle to live these prophetic words all the rest of my life. The Lord told me through her: It is not just about what you think, but about your relationship with me. Our relationship will determine how well you understand and fulfill your call, what you do and who you become. I thought to myself, how did God arrange that moment and scores of others like it?

Mother Teresa's love for Jesus was equal to any of the great saints throughout the ages. She was not naive about the severity of the love to which Christ calls us. Christ's love and loving him was not simple, sentimental love. It is strong and sacrificial, the kind of love Jesus meant when he said, "If you love those who love you, what benefit is that to you? For even sinners love those who love them."[1] Jesus was so much the embodiment of this supernatural love that he could forgive people as they hung him on a cross, though none of them even realized their need for forgiveness. His love had such great power that he spoke and healed people who were miles away, and still does.

Jesus commanded of his disciples two kinds of love that summed up the entire Ten Commandments: "You shall love the Lord your

God with all your heart and with all your soul and with all your mind. This is the great and first commandment. And a second is like it: You shall love your neighbor as yourself."[2] While most people are often comfortable with acknowledging the humanistic second commandment, Jesus was telling us, as Mother was telling me: truly, you will not be able to do the second without the first.

Mother Teresa answered her call to love the most unlovable of people. There is no reason to romanticize the poor just because we make the mistake of romanticizing the rich. The people the Missionaries serve are difficult, just as you and I are difficult, yet their needs are more desperate. The divine love of God working through her drew us; her ability to love when there was no natural reason for it attracted us to Jesus.

"We the Missionaries of Charity carry out an offensive of love, of prayer, of sacrifice on behalf of the poorest of the poor. We want to conquer the world through love, and thus bring to everyone's heart the love of God and the proof that God loves the world."[3]

This is the way Mother and the Missionaries of Charity evangelize the world: by living out the invincible, incomprehensible, almost unbearable love of Christ.

Appendix A

A Brief History of the University and Dominant Worldviews

THEOLOGIAN JAROSLAV PELIKAN WROTE, "Regardless of what anyone may personally think or believe about him, Jesus of Nazareth has been the dominant figure in the history of Western culture for almost twenty centuries. If it were possible, with some supermagnet, to pull up out of history every scrap of metal bearing at least a trace of his name, how much would be left? It is from his birthday that most of the human race dates its calendars, by his name that millions curse and in his name that millions pray."[1]

Until the late 1800s, the vast majority of universities in the West were founded on Christianity. Though Jewish and Islamic academies existed as early as Christian ones (circa 1100), they remained limited to serving their own, while Christians believed that the education of a nation was a Christian duty. Indeed, during the founding of Harvard, the Puritans even made special provision for educating Native Americans.[2] Beginning in the 1900s, most elite Protestant universities began to sever their ties with the church denominations that had developed them, becoming secular. Catholic universities largely hung on until the 1960s.[3] William Buckley brought the consequences of this to the fore in his famous treatise, *God and Man at Yale*, in 1951.[4]

George Marsden describes precisely the situation in which I and other Christian scholars find ourselves when he suggests that the very idea of Christian scholarship is viewed as outrageous in the current academy.[5] Literary scholar Kathy Bassard likens the problem to that of the Jews who, it is noted in Psalm 137, were required to sing the songs of Zion to their captors. "How shall we sing the Lord's song in a foreign land?" she asks.[6] Today, to speak of God in any serious or orthodox way in the Western academy is considered sheer foolishness, perhaps even illegal, though certainly no one could teach about the history of philosophy or the university without it.[7]

Philosophically, the West began with Augustine (circa A.D. 400) and his foundational principle that in order to understand, one must first believe. The father of modern science, Francis Bacon (circa 1600), put forward the foundational principle that science would reveal more about the mind of God, while allowing us to improve human conditions. After years of meditation, Descartes (circa 1640) gave us two famous philosophic insights: "I think, therefore I am" and "Because I am, God exists." The ordering of revelation had already begun to slip.

Scientists, both empiricists and naturalists, in the Modern Era began to believe that all knowledge must be materially verifiable—in other words, measurable through the five senses. In the nineteenth century, the human or social sciences (anthropology, sociology, psychology) eventually fully adopted Protagoras's claim (circa 400 B.C.) that man was the measure of all things. Many of today's philosophers, social scientists and humanities faculty teach that all knowledge is socially constructed and that human beings determine "truths" in the contexts of our culture and language, and the communities in which we choose to live. All knowledge becomes relative, and overarching truths (metanarratives) are no longer seen as valid. However, even these postmodern philosophies and theories have a truth statement: there are no overarching truths; there are only multiple competing "truths." This is a statement about what a person must accept on faith in order to be a progressivist or postmodernist.

The exhilaration of the Enlightenment and dawning of modernism led European and North American scholars to become so enamored with what they could know and do that they came to believe in their own wisdom and goodness. After the philosopher Kant, of the late eighteenth century, dismissed the metaphysical as unknowable, contemporary philosophers followed suit and soon no longer even engaged the question of God. Philosophers, humanists and social scientists have developed various philosophies and theories over the past century that have rejected the possibility that there is (or even could be) a living God who created and acts in the world, sustaining a relationship with humans.

Some of the philosophic movements of the last couple hundred years include empiricism, behaviorism, existentialism, nihilism, structuralism, deconstructivism, critical theory (Marxism) and postmodernism. Out of these have emerged related theories in the social sciences, including psychoanalytics, behaviorism, cognitive science, progressivism, constructivism, critical pedagogy, radical feminism and multiculturalism, and secular humanism.

Today virtually all major philosophies and theories taught in the university are devoid of God. The many Christian principles that would complete or compete with them are missing from conversations at the academic roundtable. We teach almost exclusively from post-Enlightenment secular worldviews. Few seem to notice that these theories, from the standpoint of Christian principles that address every aspect of life, are incomplete at best, gross distortions at worst.

There remains, though, incredible depth in the Christian scholars, writers, scientists, composers and artists who did not separate their understanding of God from their work. People such as these, essentially, built Western civilization.[8] These include some of our finest scientists (Copernicus, Newton, Galileo, Bacon), musicians (Bach, Beethoven, Handel), reformers (William Wilberforce, Jane Adams, Sojourner Truth, Martin Luther King Jr.), writers (Tolkien, Dostoevsky, Lewis), philosophers (Anselm, Augustine, Aquinas, Ignatius) and artists (Michelangelo, Greco, Rembrandt).

While some have proclaimed the United States and Europe "post-Christian," the West still owes most of its advance to the early application of Christian principles that were once commonly understood and shared. These include the founding principles in democracies, the humanist urge, the scientific method, the entrepreneurial spirit, the formation of musical notation, early art and literature. In the last century, some of this work has been censored to omit the faith of early Christian writers.[9] For example, contemporary books about Martin Luther King Jr. rarely refer to the scriptural principles he used to found the Civil Rights Movement. Still some of the best guides to living justly are his sermons.[10]

I began to realize that if we even considered it a possibility that Christianity contained any truth, it would be among the plethora of worldviews offered in the university. For example, there would at least be some recognition in psychology that forgiveness (God's forgiving us and our forgiving others) is as central to emotional health as vitamins are to physical health.[11] We would investigate whether praising God reduces depression[12] and whether

God causes the wealth of the unjust to transfer to those who love the poor.[13] In education, some recognition would remain that one worldview believes that fear and love of God advances wisdom. At least we would engage, among all the others, St. Peter's developmental sequence for human growth—from faith, to virtue, to knowledge, then self-control, perseverance, godliness, brotherly love and love.[14] Today knowledge is first and few have the courage to discuss faith or virtue.

Julie Reuben, in her excellent history, notes that throughout the various intellectual transformations in the Western university, the topic of morality became marginalized. She documents the moving of the moral conversation from the central-most place in the university curriculum to the theology department, then to liberalized religion departments, to moral philosophy, then science, sociology, the humanities and lastly to the dean of students office.[15] Scholar James Burtchaell wrote, "The contemporary university has . . . only primitive and emotional dealings with the Good."[16]

Philosopher Dallas Willard describes our cultural dilemma, especially within the university:

> The test of character posed by the gentleness of God's approach to us is especially dangerous for those formed by the ideas that dominate our modern world. We live in a culture that, for centuries now, has cultivated the idea that the skeptical person is always smarter than one who believes. You can be almost as stupid as a cabbage as long as you doubt. The fashion of the age has identified mental sharpness with a pose, not with genuine intellectual method and character. Only a very hardy individualist or social rebel—or one desperate for another life—therefore stands any chance of discovering the substantiality of the spiritual life today. Today, it is the skeptics who are the social conformists, though because

of powerful intellectual propaganda they continue to enjoy thinking of themselves as wildly individualistic and unbearably bright. Partly because of this social force toward skepticism, which remains very powerful even when we step into Christian congregations and colleges for ministers, very few people ever develop competence in their prayer life. . . . Today we live in a culture that overwhelmingly gives primary, if not exclusive, importance to the visible. This stance is incorporated in the power structures that permeate our world and is disseminated by the education system and government.[17]

WORLDVIEWS DOMINANT IN TODAY'S UNIVERSITY

The intellectual principles I was and was not taught shaped my own reluctance and even rebellion toward God. I was poorly educated because I was educated from very limited worldviews, which by the time I was in the university, had become sacred ideologies, secular religions. Today the limited worldviews and ideological commitments of the university are even narrower than when I went to school. Add to this the relative comfort of life in the West and the desire of all people to think of themselves as good and not needing any redemption, and you have a dangerous formula for ignorance or worse. Today, three primary worldviews dominate the university, and I was an advocate of all of them. You might say I was a naturalist and secular humanist by day and pantheist by night, not realizing their fundamental incompatibilities.

Naturalism. A fanciful story is going around that sheds some light and humor on the controversy between theistic and naturalistic views of science. After scientists mapped the human genome, a group of them decided to send a delegation to God to tell him, "Thank you very much, but we can do it all on our own now."

They went and God graciously thanked them for their information. But before they left, he asked if they might join him in a human-making contest. They agreed. God stooped down to pick up some dirt. The leader of the delegation did the same. Whereupon, God said, "No, no, you get your own dirt."

This apocryphal tale highlights the central issue: a Christian or other theist believes that man can know everything about the elements and processes that exist in the natural world through the methods of science, yet still never know anything about God—the true origin of the world and its *telos* or purpose. A Christian who is a scientist understands that these methods that work to study the natural world are extremely valuable and yet are not capable of studying the spiritual world. God stands beyond our scientific methods and instrumentation.

Naturalism is the belief that the natural, physical, material world is all there is, and that the life we now know came from much more primitive life forms that evolved over time on their own from random processes. Carl Sagan very effectively popularized this faith by beginning each episode of his television series, *The Cosmos,* standing in front of a picture of outer space saying, "The cosmos is all there is or ever was or ever will be." Little did most of us know what he was really saying, or what his beautiful-sounding language was indoctrinating us to believe about our world and ourselves.

Scientists who are religious and scientists who are naturalists all use and agree on the same methodology for understanding the natural world—the scientific method. Francis Bacon, a Christian, developed this method in the sixteenth century. Isaac Newton, one of the first presidents of the Royal Society, applied the scientific method as he conducted his work "for the glory of God." He actually wrote more in theology than science. One of the world's most prominent scientists, Francis Collins, former head of the Human

Genome Project, suggests that science reveals the language of God. He writes, "Science is the only legitimate way to investigate the natural world. . . . Science can make mistakes. But the nature of science is self-correcting. . . . Nevertheless, science alone is not enough to answer all the important questions. . . . Science is not the only way of knowing. The spiritual worldview provides another way of finding truth. Scientists who deny this would be well advised to consider the limits of their own tools."[18]

British theologian and missionary Lesslie Newbigin argued that those of us who live in a world dominated by science must work to understand other ways of thinking. "As people who are part of modern Western culture, with its confidence in the validity of its scientific methods, how can we move from the place where we explain the gospel in terms of our modern scientific world-view to the place where we explain our modern scientific world-view from the point of view of the gospel?" He states the reality plainly, "The Christian claim is that, though [the Christian worldview] can in no way be reached by any logical step from the axioms of [the scientific worldview], nevertheless [the Christian worldview] does offer a wider rationality that embraces and does not contradict the rationality of the [scientific worldview]."[19] This was my experience. From the worldviews in which I had put my faith, I could not understand the Christian worldview. However, from the Christian worldview, I could understand with greater clarity even my previous worldviews.

The strict naturalist believes that scientific methods ultimately will answer all our questions, and supernatural explanations are unnecessary and wrongheaded. Such scientists hold that there is no reason to believe in any other force in the universe other than random natural processes. The new fanatical, evangelical atheists, such as Richard Dawkins, Daniel Dennett, Christopher Hitchens and Sam Harris, are all frequent speakers in the university.[20] Most of them are naturalists and secular humanists. Though little engaged in the actual practice of scientific inquiry, they argue vociferously against the idea that God created the world, exists beyond scientific scrutiny and continues to act in the world.

These are essentially the same arguments against God and spiritual reality that have existed since the beginning of recorded history. David and Solomon in 900 B.C. encountered them. Plato argued against members of the Protagorian school about the same naturalistic arguments in 400 B.C. Paul encountered them in the Epicureans in A.D. 40 in Athens. Almost eight hundred years ago, theologian Thomas Aquinas systematically contradicted these naturalistic fallacies in his monumental theological treatise on God *(Summa Theologica)*, describing God as the unmoved mover, the uncaused cause, the incorruptible being that leads us to know good, and the intelligent designer (orderer) of the universe who stands both beyond and in time.[21]

Some scientists cling to the purely naturalistic Darwinian theory to explain the evolution of the natural world, in particular the emergence of the human being. While plenty of scientific evidence exists of evolution within species, there is still scant evidence to support the evolution of one species into another.[22] Yet there are both Christians and non-Christians who believe in some form of evolution, theistic or otherwise.[23] Science and Christianity are completely compatible, indeed modern science emerged from Christianity. Today there are many more Christians who are professors of science than there are Christian professors of the social sciences and the humanities.

The major intellectual debate that continues to this day is between naturalists, who believe that natural phenomenon is all there is, and those who believe, like Francis Collins, "in the complementary nature of the scientific and spiritual worldviews." He writes, "Science is not threatened by God; it is enhanced. God is most certainly not threatened by science; He made it all possible. . . . That ancient motherland of reason and worship was never in danger of crumbling. It never will be."[24] However, the media tends to distort the disagreements between scientists who believe in God and naturalists; the media tries to depict the disagreements as between six-day creationists and "real" scientists.[25] That is simply not the case. Both groups are scientists, and the major debate is over a purely naturalistic worldview and its assault on ways of knowing outside of the scientific method, as well as its insistence that the material world is all there is.

Why does the naturalism debate center so heavily around naturalistic evolution? I believe it is because the idea of evolution not only undergirds naturalism but secular humanism as well. It suggests both (1) that nature and the random processes such as natural selection are sufficient explanations of all life, and (2) that human beings are becoming better and better every day—not just physically but socially and morally as well, a process sometimes called social Darwinism. It fits very well into the post-Enlightenment paradigm where human beings are seen as fully capable—without the help of a living God—to create and sustain a peaceful, loving, technologically supreme one-world.

Secular humanism. Secular humanism holds a utopian view of human nature. During the Renaissance, humanism was compatible with Christianity; it was associated with an increased optimism in human achievement and possibilities, and the value of a classical liberal arts education. By the twentieth century, those who rejected religious transcendence had captured the term *humanism*.[26] The humanism undergirding dominant ideas in the social sciences and humanities today is secular *humanism*. Some secular humanists are also naturalists and some are not, but both groups exclude God and focus on human potentiality. Christopher

Hitchens, the atheist journalist who wrote critically of Mother Teresa, and Paul Kurtz, founder and director of the Council for Secular Humanism, are two prominent fundamentalist advocates for secular humanism.

In the discussion of secular humanism that is offered by Paul Kurtz and his council, he says of atheism and secular humanism:

> Secular humanists do not rely upon gods or other super-natural forces to solve their problems or provide guidance for their conduct. They rely instead upon the application of reason, the lessons of history, and personal experience to form an ethical/moral foundation and to create meaning in life. . . . [T]heir cosmic outlook draws primarily from human experience and scientific knowledge.[27]

As a former secular humanist, trusting in my human experience and scientific knowledge to determine morality for living my life had disastrous consequences both for me and others. Human reason in the absence of a worldview that defines goodness as something more than what a bunch of us can come up with is easily infected not with reason, but with rationalization. The rationalizing mind cannot distinguish its thoughts from reason. I could rationalize having sexual relationships with a married man with any number of "human reasons"—his marriage was on the rocks, his wife did not really love him, it's not really hurting anyone . . . the list was endless. I could use illegal drugs because, after all, it only hurt me (though I did not really believe it would, and a few "scientific discoveries" were always available to reassure me on this one). Peter Singer, a famous "ethicist" at Princeton University, believes that we should be able to euthanize newborns up to three to four weeks after birth if for some reason we don't get what we want. He uses reason to argue for this. Should you think this is some eccentric example, note that his book *Practical Ethics* has been voted one of the most influential books in twentieth-century philosophy.[28]

Combining scientific knowledge with human experience proves problematic. For example, the latest manual on mental deficiency lowered the seriousness of the classification of pedophilia. It is judged a clinical problem if the urges "cause clinically significant distress or impairment in social, occupational or other important areas of functioning."[29] Because psychiatry no longer has any clear or permanent boundaries for discerning normal from abnormal behavior, as particular human behaviors become more prevalent, they become normalized. Naturalism and human experience together will construct a world where humans determine right and wrong, good and evil, from statistics on how many people approve of or engage in the behavior. Our parents' common sense told them the danger of this. When my sisters and I wanted to do something that our mother or father resisted, we would use the same reasoning, though we didn't know we were using statistical arguments. We would protest, "But Mom, Dad, everyone is doing it." Our parents would reply that they did not care if everyone was doing it, we would not.

In the Christian worldview, a set of moral standards and ways of best being in the world stands outside us. Just as the inventor of a machine has regulations and procedures for its optimal performance, so does God for the world he created. It is not left to us to determine moral values but to obey the principles we have been given. We are responsible for obeying and confessing when we fail in order that we might be transformed and made more able to work toward our destiny. Within the principles of Christianity that we are to obey, there are endless possibilities for unique and widely variant personalities, cultures, languages, styles, skills, interests, experiences and life purposes.

Panentheism/spiritualism. In the West, at the beginning of the nineteenth century, romanticists and transcendentalists co-opted characteristics of God, such as goodness and transcendence, and made them descriptive of human nature. Pantheism is the idea that humans are spiritual, sentient beings who are, or with work can be, one with nature and divine like God/gods. This is accomplished by working to connect to and magnify energy for personal spiritual power.

Pantheism, or spirituality or spiritualism, is becoming the rage on university campuses. Both the Eastern religions and New Age movement are examples of pantheism. These also fit well with secular humanists' and naturalists' optimism about human potential. A pantheist may also be an enthusiast of science. Indeed, there are a number of scientists and engineers who experiment with paranormal phenomena, which is how I became involved. (However, a strict naturalist would not be a pantheist per se, as they would deny the supernatural. But both naturalists and pantheists tend to believe in secular humanism.)

Shirley MacLaine popularized the pantheistic worldview with her descriptions of past lives and spirit guides. Deepak Chopra and Sai Baba are other popular pantheists. Hinduism and Buddhism are pantheistic religions. When adherents of these faiths consider Christ, they see Jesus as a man, a wise philosopher, but not as the Son of God, the Messiah, though he did not leave us this option as he claimed to be the Son of God. C. S. Lewis pointed out he either was who he said he was or he was a madman.[30] More recently Rhonda Byrne has popularized "spirituality."

Pantheism's popularity is evident in the fact that today you can buy things like yoga mats, Eastern meditation music and statues of Buddha in Target. Markets follow the prevailing worldviews and preferences of the times. When I was a graduate student in the university in the 1970s, pantheistic opportunities were primarily extracurricular activities. I explored transcendental meditation, hallucinogenic drugs and marijuana, Zen, bending spoons, white witchcraft and more in order to reach my higher self, to become more "spiritual." I always equated becoming more spiritual with becoming good, but of course every religion recognizes that evil is also spiritual.

Buddhism is the most respected religion in the university and is quite compatible with prevalent secular philosophies and theories in the social sciences and humanities, where pantheistic principles are now frequently embedded in classes and in class assignments. I see a number of students who have grown up in Christian homes become enamored with pantheism's "spiritual" promises when they get to the university. I believe that this is because Western Christianity has tended to downplay the mystical aspects of Christ and Christianity in preference for the more intellectual ones. We have explained the gospel in terms of Western scientific thinking. Young adults who are interested in and believe in spiritual phenomena and realities are easily led away to the mystical promises of many pantheists, as I was. So while studies may report that students become more spiritual in college,[31] they generally become less Christian.

Scholar James Herrick defines the differences between Christianity and the new spiritualities as the difference between belief in the "revealed word" and revelation from a living and personal God versus "the new religious synthesis," and "human discovery."[32] The spiritual hunger of today's university students (and professors) is evident in their searching, and searching is not a bad thing. Everyone must own their own faith; no one can depend on another's, whether it be faith in naturalism, Buddhism, humanism or Christianity.

Christ said that, to follow him, we have to be "born again."[33]

We have to make that decision for ourselves; our parents cannot do it for us. We can be born to parents who follow Christ, but ultimately, to be a Christian, an individual must commit his or her life to God. Once this rebirth happens, the transformations of body, soul and spirit begin to move us more surely toward the good, the healthy, the wise, and to all that we need to know to fulfill our destiny—and to more fully experience the love and grace of God.

If the university is going to teach spiritual worldviews, and I believe it should, it should do so more consciously and even-handedly. Secularizing the university was to produce an intellectual openness and vitality; thus far, it has had a more reductionistic and dulling effect. Once I got to the university, I was steered away from Christianity by people who knew nothing of it, and who taught that it was evil, naive or simply irrelevant. Since I had never really studied it or made it my own, it was easy to get lost in a plethora of vague platitudes about spirituality, goodness and pantheistic proselytizing. I then perpetuated my ignorance on my students.

One of the major distinctions in my being "spiritual but not religious" was that I could not or would not deal with evil, especially evil inside myself. Being spiritual and not religious allowed me to select the spiritual assumptions that best fit my lifestyle at the moment. The amorphous "spirituality" I developed did not distinguish one religion from another, so I was free to choose cafeteria-style from multiple religions and spiritual frameworks. One day I might choose Zen precepts, the next some other precept from the New Age movement, which would make me feel I was good while I was living a life that was bad. My "spirituality" was actually more closely linked to my emotions and, secondarily, to my mind than to my spirit. Certainly, my spirit was disconnected from the Spirit of God. I thought myself most "spiritual" when I felt the best about myself. When I used to tell Christians that I was "spiritual but not religious," I was essentially asserting that I was better (more advanced spiritually) than them because I did not need such rigid structures to be "good."

There was an outward look of peace and serene joy in my pantheism, but underneath it, all kinds of chaos reigned inside me. Never did my individualism and self-centeredness have freer reign. We were all young and healthy, working unceasingly on ourselves and our own enlightenment. As a Christian, I am called to work on myself as an individual in need of Christ's redemption and to work in a world that is in need of the same. I am a body and a soul with a mind, will and emotions. The Holy Spirit works in my spirit and through my mind (i.e., my conscience, intuition, revelation, reason, etc.).

From a Christian worldview, all things are made of things not seen—the spiritual. Our relationship with Christ allows us access to God (to be children of God) and grants that the Holy Spirit will be our guide and comforter. But there are other spirits as well, and not all spirits are holy or good, as evil is also spiritual. Paul refers to these spirits as the powers and principalities of the air.[34] The spiritual realm that is part of the world in which we live leads either to light or to dark, good or evil. God's precepts and principles, as embodied in Christ and empowered through the Holy Spirit, allow us to work for good to the degree that we can hear and cooperate with his guidance.

In our own lives, we battle constantly to act on the principles and guidance of God for good or to act for evil. God's Holy Spirit is crucial, because there are things that from our natural eyes look "good" but do not lead to life. Our relationship with Christ is always leading us to the right path and to be aware of and reject the evil desires that also draw us. The recognition of our sins is not to lead us to live a guilt-ridden life but to come to the freedom that only redemption and self-knowledge can give us, to overcome evil and choose good. The true Christian life is profoundly mystical.

DOMINANT WORLDVIEWS AND CHRISTIANITY

From a Christian worldview, there are truths inside every world-view, yet each is flawed (as each of these would also see the Christian worldview as flawed). Like the naturalist, the Christian worldview wholly supports efforts in science to improve the human condition and care for all creation, but it doesn't believe that the scientific method is capable of locating or studying God. A Christian does not believe the world is composed solely of natural phenomena; a Christian does believe that even our ability to study natural phenomena is a God-given gift

Christians also share the humanists' goals to love and help one another and build peaceful communities; after all, Christ's second commandment is to love your neighbor as yourself. However, Christians do not believe we are capable of doing this fully without first loving God with all our heart and mind and soul—the first commandment. Our service to others is most helpful when done within the boundaries of these principles.

Furthermore, a Christian clearly believes, as pantheists do, that the spiritual world exists and operates behind natural phenomena. But Christians do not agree that humans and nature are divine, or that we can perfect our own enlightenment. Rather, the way of redemption and healthy growth comes from God working in our weakness and through spiritual disciplines, such as prayer, confession and worship.

SUMMARY

The absence of Christian perspectives has diminished the university's own commitment to academic freedom and to providing universal education. When the worldview of Christianity is lost in the larger public conversation, it becomes increasingly trivialized and privatized. This is so pandemic that the founders of the new European Union wrote their constitution without any reference to Christianity in the history of Europe, a fact that Pope John Paul II, Benedict XVI and others have worked to correct. Even atheist philosopher Jurgen Habermas has argued against the absence of Christianity in the history—not because he is a believer, but because he loves the truth. Habermas said, "Christianity, and nothing else, is the ultimate foundation of liberty, conscience, human rights, and democracy, the benchmarks of Western civilization."[35]

Appendix B

Toward a Twenty-First-Century University

For the time is coming when people will not endure sound teaching,
but having itching ears they will accumulate for themselves
teachers to suit their own passions, and will turn away
from listening to the truth and wander off into myths.

2 TIMOTHY 4:3-4

⚛

POSTMODERN LITERARY THEORIST, and popular commentator on the university scene, Stanley Fish shocked the university in 2005 by suggesting that the intellectual rush was over for high theory, culture and gender studies, and that the baton had moved to religion, "where the action is."[1] He warned the academy that it had better get ready. This clarion call speaks to both nonsectarian and religious colleges and universities.

Contrary to popular myth, secular higher education in the West does censor the worldviews it teaches. Historian John Som-

merville believes that the many years of secularism have made
the university increasingly marginal to American society and that
"secular ideals" are no guarantee of an absence of bias, just different ones.[2] Biases in higher education curricula come in two forms:
what is privileged and what is ignored and/or despised. Abraham
Heschel argued that he did not so much oppose secularization as
the way secularity had reduced the academy.[3]

I am not suggesting that nonsectarian universities and colleges
are going to go back and restore their Christian foundations, but I
am saying that the absence of a worldview as significant to world
history, science and human progress as Christianity leaves a tremendous void in the curriculum of higher education. However,
the nonsectarian university could begin to restore its commitment
to providing universal education by teaching all worldviews.

Universities and their faculty need to become conscious and
intentional about articulating the foundational principles of all
worldviews (those it considers religious or secular). This would
require the reeducation of faculty and a new approach to educating future scholars, thus a new approach to graduate education.

Most of us have gone to graduate school in reductionistic en-
vironments, rarely contemplating the foundational principles
upon which our fields are currently based, simply accepting them
unself-consciously.[4] Scholar James Sire says, "For any of us to be
fully conscious intellectually we should not only be able to detect
the worldviews of others but be aware of our own—why it is ours
and why in light of so many options we think it is true."[5]

This new university would intentionally hire people who can
adequately articulate these views; not just people who study them
intellectually or critique them. Augustine's distinction between
understanding the material and the spiritual worlds is paramount
here: "There are some things, which we do not believe unless we
understand them [material, scientific], and there are other things

which we do not understand unless we believe them [spiritual]."[6] There is no question in my mind that I could not, as a nonbeliever, have understood the Christian worldview, except in a shallow, textbook way, and other nonbelievers do not understand it either.

The twenty-first-century university, or a department within the university, may choose to make a conscious decision to omit one or more worldviews, or it may take a stand to teach only one. In that case, it should clearly say so in its mission statement.

TOWARD A TWENTY-FIRST-CENTURY CHRISTIAN GRADUATE UNIVERSITY

Write the vision;
make it plain on tablets,
so he may run who reads it.
For still the vision awaits its appointed time;
it hastens to the end—it will not lie.
If it seems slow, wait for it;
it will surely come; it will not delay. (Habakkuk 2:2-3)

Christians have an enormous opportunity and responsibility here. To "get ready," in Fish's terms, Christians must engage the academic world even more seriously, deeply and rigorously. Undergraduate colleges and universities that have kept their orthodox foundations do work to prepare undergraduates to discern foundational principles of worldviews and prepare them for entry into professional work or graduate school. And many of these colleges and universities also offer master's programs. Some of the largest of these offer even more extensive graduate work, but by and large, many have lost their orthodox Christian distinctiveness. Reinvigorating orthodoxy in established Christian colleges is essential, as well as increasing the number of rigorous, high quality, orthodox graduate programs in every field.

They were to be educated for three years. . . . As for these four youths, God gave them learning and skill in all literature and wisdom, and Daniel had understanding in all visions and dreams. At the end of the time . . . in every matter of wisdom and understanding about which the king inquired of them, he found them ten times better than all the magicians and enchanters that were in all his kingdom. (Daniel 1:5, 17-18, 20)

The penultimate call for Christians interested in higher education is to develop a series of stand-alone, but connected, graduate universities that would be thoroughly orthodox, from their founding boards to their staff, to their finances, to their scientific and artistic contributions, to their daily schedule, to their use of land and on and on. Principles of the gospel would form the foundational vision of these new graduate universities. These universities would be all over the world and linked to one another, committing themselves to work directly on the pivotal needs for the twenty-first century.

You are the light of the world. A city set on a hill cannot be hidden. Nor do people light a lamp and put it under a basket, but on a stand, and it gives light to all in the house. In the same way, let your light shine before others, so that they may see your good works and give glory to your Father who is in heaven. (Matthew 5:14-16)

Because Christ calls us to redemptive work in the world, these graduate universities should focus directly on the needs of the twenty-first-century culture. Working in interdisciplinary groups, faculty and students (and concerned intercessors) would tackle the particularly thorny problems in this century. Some of the issues that come easily to mind include economical desalinization; clean and safe energy sources; cures that stimulate healthy body functions to overcome disease; educating the poor; building new, more equitable and productive economic systems; stimulating new enthusiasm and beauty in music, art and literature; and government that truly encourages the virtue of nations and their citizens . . . the list is endless.

In my Father's house are many rooms. (John 14:2)

Behold, how good and pleasant it is
*   when brothers dwell in unity!*
For there the LORD has commanded the blessing,
*   life forevermore. (Psalm 133:1, 3)*

People drawn from the entire orthodox body of Christ would unite in these graduate centers, forming graduate universities that are multidenominational, international and crosscultural. So rather than being denominationally and nationally based (as current Christian colleges are), believers who are orthodox in their foundational beliefs—from Catholic, Protestant, Eastern Orthodox, Messianic traditions—would come together to work. Without this, the body in academia remains divided, and our revelation, wisdom and blessing are limited. I wonder if this is why Mark Noll finds that evangelicals are less viable intellectually[7] —we have too severely narrowed access to the mind of God by constricting Christian colleges by denominational doctrines.

Now concerning spiritual gifts, brothers, I do not want you to be uninformed. . . . Now there are varieties of gifts, but the same Spirit; and there are varieties of service, but the same Lord; and there are varieties of activities, but it is the same God who empowers them all in everyone. To each is given the manifestation of the Spirit for the common good. . . . But God has so composed the body, giving greater honor to the part that lacked it, that there may be no division in the body, but that the members may have the same care for one another. (1 Corinthians 12:1, 4-7, 24-25)

A second aspect of the body of Christ, taken from Scripture, is that different people have different giftings. In a vital Christian university, all gifts must be activated—intellectual, prophtic, discernment, intercession, healing, mercy and so on. Not everyone involved in the work of the graduate university will be an academic; we must have many varieties of gifts in the body of Christ in order to optimally conduct the work. There must be a consciousness and openness to the possibility that the gardener may have an essential prophetic word for the researcher, or that a team of intercessors may spearhead a critical, revelatory breakthrough for a group of scientists.

I appeal to you therefore, brothers, by the mercies of God, to present your bodies as a living sacrifice, holy and acceptable to God, which is your spiritual worship. Do not be conformed to this world, but be transformed by the renewal of your mind, that by testing you may discern what is the will of God, what is good and acceptable and perfect. (Romans 12:1-2)

Faculty and administrators will need strong gifts and skills of discernment of foundational principles of their fields and of Christian intellectual principles. As faculty who are Christians, we would need to seriously search Scripture and seek new revelation for insights and discoveries in our disciplines and among them (transdisciplinary work). We would need to take Scripture and revelation as seriously as the latest journal.

And it shall come to pass afterward,
*   that I will pour out my Spirit on all flesh;*
your sons and your daughters shall prophesy,
*   your old men shall dream dreams,*

and your young men shall see visions.
Even on the male and female servants
in those days I will pour out my Spirit. *(Joel 2:28-29)*

These new graduate universities will serve a critical role as a sabbatical site for faculty who are Christians and scholars but have never had the time nor the counsel to discern the application of Christian principles to their fields. The twenty-first-century university will be fruitful only if we are intentional, strategic and enthusiastic about designing vigorous and rigorous alternatives to what currently exists in both secular and Christian colleges. Graduates of these universities could take their places alongside colleagues of other worldviews or among Christians. They would join the ranks of the most highly educated, having a clear understanding of their own worldview, as well as of the alternatives, knowing how to seek and hear the wisdom of God, in addition to being able to understand the many years of gathered insights from their fields. Like Daniel we should be found ten times wiser. Such a graduate university would be a great step toward fulfilling Isaiah's prophecy:

They shall build up the ancient ruins;
    they shall raise up the former devastations;
they shall repair the ruined cities,
    the devastations of many generations. (Isaiah 61:4)

Acknowledgments

I F I WERE TRULY TO ACKNOWLEDGE all those who have signifi-
cantly helped me along this path, it would take a very, very
long chapter. I would want to start by listing all those who
ever said a prayer for me before or since my desire to follow
Christ and for the author of every book I read that helped me,
and every homily, sermon or teaching that ever encouraged me
and there were many indeed. Sadly, I would not even know all
their names.

So many from the various denominations in Christ's body have
taught me. I am particularly grateful to:

Mother Teresa and the Missionaries of Charity.

The sisters, brothers and priests (past and present) of Pecos
Benedictine Monastery, and to Father Angelo Scolozzi (Mexico).

To those who helped me find my way to Calcutta—Marjorie
and Will Sukow, Mitra and Swapan Nag, Neepa Chowdhury, Syng
Yu, and Goudi Bose and Dana, my fellow volunteer.

To the innumerable laborers in Campus Crusade, InterVarsity, Chi Alpha and Newman Centers who selflessly contribute their gifts and prayers. To the students who pray for campus renewal.

Special thanks to Dan Cho, executive director of Veritas Forum, for taking the manuscript on a plane one day and handing it over to InterVarsity Press, and to the founder of Veritas Forums, Kelly Monroe Kullberg, for her wisdom, support and encouragement.

To my brilliant and witty colleagues at the Tuesday Lunch Group for their fellowship and their generosity and wisdom in reviewing a portion of the manuscript.

To Bob and Barbara Eagleton, Ann Geerken, Dorothy Steele, Maureen Brians, Thuy Huynh, Charlotte Carpena, Bill and Becky Hitt, Ursula and John West, Irene Lund, Randy and Cheryl Lee, Gerri Morris, Beverly Chen, Phyllis Jones, Betty June Thompson, Johanna Sharp, Julie De Lavergne, Jamie Caridi, Bea and Art Cleveland, Bill and Martha Forti—all prayerful friends to whom I am most grateful. To my loving, long-time friend Ruth Greene, for her wit, intelligence and artistic sensibilities.

Special thanks to the board, administration, faculty and staff at Claremont Graduate University and to my terrific students who constantly keep me learning and laughing.

To a fabulous editor, Al Hsu, whose steady guidance, grace, peace and patience were both remarkable and invaluable, and to those who worked alongside him: Taryn Bullis, Cindy Kiple, Ruth Curphey, Tabitha Plueddemann, Elaina Whittenhall and Betsy Conlin.

To my marvelous sisters: Jane and her husband, Rick Landrum, and my niece Melissa and nephew Brian and their families (James, Brynea, and their children Hayden, Bella, Cole and Parker) for love, delicious meals and joy. To my sister Anne for the many years of extraordinary love and prayers. To my sister Sue and her husband, Warren King, who opened their home and cooked elegant meals when I went for respite.

Last, but surely not least, two people in my life who prove the Proverb "the sweetness of a friend comes from his earnest counsel."

To Sandra Seymour for her unfailing friendship and prayers. Thank you for always showing me, by example, where to place my feet so that I may better follow the Holy Spirit.

And to John Rivera, for the gargantuan wisdom he shares about all of life. Without his wisdom, faithfulness and tenacity, my mind would have continued to grow more confused, and I would have never realized my need for or the way of redemption.

May God repay them all one hundredfold!

Notes

≥≡≤

Introduction: Telling the Truth About Mother Teresa

[1]Ann and Jeanette Petrie, *Mother Teresa* (Canada: Petrie Productions, 1986). This documentary film is narrated by Richard Attenborough and covers the work of Mother Teresa and the Missionaries over five years in ten countries. It includes many interviews with Mother Teresa and those close to her. It is distributed by Ignatius Press.

[2]Malcolm Muggeridge, *Something Beautiful for God* (New York: Image Books, 1977). Among the books about Mother Teresa published by Servant Publications are *Jesus the Word to be Spoken, Heart of Joy, One Heart Full of Love, Total Surrender, Thirsting for God, Loving Jesus,* and *Suffering into Joy.* These books are available from St. Anthony Messenger Press.

[3]Abraham Heschel, *The Prophets* (New York: Harper Torchbooks, 1962), pp. xii-xiii.

[4]Edward Le Joly, *Mother Teresa: A Woman in Love* (Notre Dame, Ind.: Ave Maria Press, 1993); Navin Chawla, *Mother Teresa: The Authorized Biography* (Boston: Element Books, 1992); Kathryn Spink, *Mother Teresa: A Complete Authorized Biography* (San Francisco: HarperSanFrancisco, 1997); Sebastian Vazhakala, *Life with Mother Teresa* (Ann Arbor, Mich.: Servant, 2004); Eileen Egan, *Such a Vision of the Streets* (U.K.: New English Library, 1986).

Chapter 2: A Day in the Life of a Missionary of Charity

[1]Malcolm Muggeridge, *Something Beautiful for God* (New York: Image Books, 1977), p. 92.

[2]Philip Jenkins, *The Next Christendom* (Oxford: Oxford University Press, 2002), p. 183.

[3]Throughout the book, I will use the term *West* and *Western* as it commonly refers to standards and thought patterns dominant in Europe, Great Britain and the United States, even though it is a misnomer. It would be more accurate to refer to it as the northwest for it clearly excludes the southern zones.

[4]Adoration is a time of prayerful adoration and reflection on the Lord in the presence of the Eucharist.

[5]Father Angelo Scolozzi, personal communication, Pecos Benedictine Monastery, August 11, 2003.

[6]José Luis González-Balado, ed., *Loving Jesus* (Ann Arbor, Mich.: Servant, 1991), pp. 35-36.

Chapter 3: A Pencil in God's Hand

[1]Brian Kolodiejchuk, *Mother Teresa, Come Be My Light: The Private Writings of the "Saint of Calcutta"* (New York: Doubleday, 2007).

[2]Ibid., p. 132.

[3]Malcolm Muggeridge, *Something Beautiful for God* (New York: Image Books, 1977), p. 14.

[4]Mother Teresa, *A Gift for God* (San Francisco: HarperSanFrancisco, 1996), p. 30.

[5]José Luis González-Balado, *Mother Teresa: In My Own Words* (New York: Gramercy Book, 1996), p. 35.

[6]*Viva Christo Rey* (Dallas: Catholic Charismatic Service of Dallas, 1981). This is a video documentary of the work of Jesuit priest Rick Thomas, Sister Mary Virginia Clark and others in El Paso/Juarez. The work began around the Scripture: "When you give a dinner or a banquet, do not invite your friends or your brothers or your relatives or rich neighbors, lest they also invite you in return and you be repaid. But when you give a feast, invite the poor, the crippled, the lame, the blind, and you will be blessed, because they cannot repay you" (Luke 14:12-14). The projects feed the poor, tend the sick and visit prisoners, as well as help the poor establish businesses and cooperatives, such as the "Lord's Store" and the "Lord's Ranch." This ministry has been the site of any number of documented miracles including the multiplication of food and healing.

[7]Galatians 2:19-20: "For through the law I died to the law, so that I might live to God. I have been crucified with Christ. It is no longer I who live, but Christ who lives in me. And the life I now live in the flesh I live by faith in the Son of God, who loved me and gave himself for me."

[8]Brother Angelo Devananda (Scolozzi), *Contemplative in the Heart of the World* (New York: Fount, 1985), p. 53.

[9]Raghu Rai and Navin Chawla, *Faith and Compassion: The Life and Work of Mother Teresa* (Rockport, Mass.: Element, 1996), p. 98.

[10]Bernard of Clairvaux *The Steps of Humility and Pride* (Kalamazoo, Mich.: Cistercian Publications, 1989), p. 30.

[11]Colossians 1:29.

[12]Rai and Chawla, *Faith and Compassion*, p. 117.

Chapter 4: Whatever You Did for the Least of These, You Did for Me

[1]Matthew 25:35-40: "'For I was hungry and you gave me food, I was thirsty and you gave me drink, I was a stranger and you welcomed me, I was naked and you clothed me, I was sick and you visited me, I was in prison and you came to me.' Then the righteous will answer him, saying, 'Lord, when did we see you hungry and feed you, or thirsty and give you drink? And when did we see you a stranger and welcome you, or naked and clothe you? And when did we see you sick or in prison and visit you?' And the King will answer them, 'Truly, I say to you, as you did it to one of the least of these my brothers, you did it to me.'"

[2]Raghu Rai and Navin Chawla, *Faith and Compassion: The Life and Work of Mother Teresa* (Rockport, Mass.: Element, 1996), p. 38.

[3]Brother Lawrence of the Resurrection, *The Practice of the Presence of God* (New York: Image Books, 1977).

[4]Malcolm Muggeridge, *Something Beautiful for God* (New York: Image Books, 1977), p. 38.

[5]Mother Teresa, *A Gift for God* (San Francisco: HarperSanFrancisco, 1996), p. 57.

[6]Rai and Chawla, *Faith and Compassion*, p. 107.

Chapter 5: The Church as Flawed and Finite

[1]Mother Teresa, *A Gift for God* (San Francisco: HarperSanFrancisco, 1996), p. 17.

[2]C. S. Lewis, *Mere Christianity* (New York: Collier/Macmillan, 1952), p. 163.

[3]Romans 2:1-5: "Therefore you have no excuse, O man, every one of you who judges. For in passing judgment on another you condemn yourself, because you, the judge, practice the very same things. We know that the judgment of God rightly falls on those who practice such things. Do you suppose, O man—you who judge those who practice such things and yet do them yourself—that you will escape the judgment of God? Or do you presume on the riches of his kindness and forbearance and patience, not knowing that God's kindness is meant to lead you to repentance? But because of your hard and impenitent heart you are storing up wrath for yourself on the day of wrath when God's righteous judgment will be revealed."

[4]1 John 1:9: "If we confess our sins, he is faithful and just to forgive us our sins and to cleanse us from all unrighteousness."

[5]Romans 7:21-25: "So I find it to be a law that when I want to do right, evil lies close at hand. For I delight in the law of God, in my inner being, but I see in my members another law waging war against the law of my mind and making me captive to the law of sin that dwells in my members. Wretched man that I am! Who will deliver me from this body of death? Thanks be to God through Jesus Christ our Lord! So then, I myself serve the law of God with my mind, but with my flesh I serve the law of sin."

Chapter 6: Do All Things Without Complaining or Disputing

[1]Watchman Nee, *The Spiritual Man*, vols. 1-3 (New York: Christian Fellowship Publishers, 1977).

[2]Philippians 2:14-15.

[3]Angelo D. Scolozzi, *Thirsting for God: A Yearbook of Prayers and Meditations* (Ann Arbor, Mich.: Saint Anthony Messenger Press and Franciscan Communications, 2000).

[4]1 Thessalonians 5:16-18.

Chapter 7: It All Belongs to God

[1]Brother Angelo Devananda (Scolozzi), *Contemplative in the Heart of the World* (New York: Fount, 1985), p. 117.

[2]Raghu Rai and Navin Chawla, *Faith and Compassion: The Life and Work of Mother Teresa* (Rockport, Mass.: Element, 1996), p. 93.

[3]Psalm 37:8: "Refrain from anger, and forsake wrath! Fret not yourself; it tends only to evil."

Chapter 8: There Is Always Enough

[1]Raghu Rai and Navin Chawla, *Faith and Compassion: The Life and Work of Mother Teresa* (Rockport, Mass.: Element, 1996), p. 101.

[2]Ibid., p. 118.

[3]Christopher Hitchens, *The Missionary Position* (New Dehli: Indus/HarperCollins, 1995).

[4]"Wealth gained hastily will dwindle, but whoever gathers little by little will increase it" (Proverbs 13:11 ESV); or "He who increases his wealth by exorbitant interest amasses it for another, who will be kind to the poor" (Proverbs 28:8 NIV).

[5]Proverbs 13:22: "A good man leaves an inheritance to his children's children, but the sinner's wealth is laid up for the righteous."

[6]Jean-Pierre de Caussade, *Abandonment to Divine Providence* (New York: Image Books, 1975), pp. 59, 51.

[7]José Luis González-Balado, *One Heart Full of Joy* (Ann Arbor, Mich.: Servant, 1984), p. 44.

Chapter 9: The Vow of Poverty and Service to the Poor

[1]A carpet of burlap covered the floor upon my arrival but was removed as the heat of summer increased, giving us a cool place on the concrete to sit and kneel during Mass.

[2]Airlines occasionally gave Mother and Missionaries free tickets. Some required her to sit in first class because of the traffic jams she caused in the aisles when she would travel in the more crowded coach.

[3]Tudor Bismarck, an African Christian Missionary who frequently ministers in the United States, made this comment in a television interview on Trinity Broadcast Network in April, 1998.

[4]Susan Conroy, *Mother Teresa: Lessons of Love and Secrets of Sanctity* (Huntington, Ind.: Our Sunday Visitor Publishing, 2003), p. 208.

[5]David B. Brinkerhoff, Lynn K. White, Suzanne Ortega and Rose Weitz, *Essentials of Sociology* (Belmont, Calif.: Wadsworth, 2005), p. 336.

[6]Philip Jenkins, *The Next Christendom: The Coming of Global Christianity* (Oxford: Oxford University Press, 2002).

[7]Malcolm Muggeridge, *Something Beautiful for God* (New York: Image Books, 1977), p. 91.

[8]From The Constitution of the Missionaries of Charity. Used with permission. Sr. Nirmala, Superior General, March 8, 2008.

[9]Germaine Greer, quoted in Robit Brijnath, Udayan Namboodiri and Ruben Bannerjee, "A Mission Ends," *India Today,* September 15, 1997.
[10]Ibid.

Chapter 10: The Vow of Obedience

[1]From the Constitution of the Missionaries of Charity. Used with permission by Sr. Nirmala, Superior General, March 8, 2008.
[2]Navin Chawla, *Mother Teresa: The Authorized Biography* (Boston: Element, 1996), p. 21.
[3]From the Constitution of the Missionaries of Charity. Used with permission. Sr. Nirmala, Superior General, March 8, 2008.
[4]Mother Teresa and Angelo Scolozzi, *Total Surrender* (Ann Arbor, Mich.: Saint Anthony Messenger Press and Franciscan Communications, 1985), pp. 71-72.
[5]Ibid., p. 73.
[6]Quoted in Malcolm Muggeridge, *Something Beautiful for God* (New York: Image Books, 1977), p. 27.

Chapter 11: The Vow of Chastity

[1]From the Constitution of the Missionaries of Charity. Used with permission, granted by Sr. Nirmala, Superior General, March 8, 2008.
[2]Mother Teresa and Angelo Scolozzi, *Total Surrender* (Ann Arbor, Mich.: Saint Anthony Messenger Press and Franciscan Communications, 1985), pp. 63, 65.
[3]Jorge Cardinal Medina Estévez, *Male and Female He Created Them: On Marriage and the Family* (San Francisco: Ignatius Press, 1997), p. 73. See also Al Hsu, *Singles at the Crossroads* (Downers Grove, Ill.: InterVarsity Press, 1997).
[4]Estévez, *Male and Female,* p. 72.
[5]Ibid., pp. 70-71. Estévez quotes a lovely passage from the apocryphal Book of Tobit, where Tobias prays to the Lord with his new wife: "Blessed are you, O God of our fathers, and blessed be your holy and glorious name for ever. Let the heavens and all your creatures bless you. You made Adam and gave him Eve his wife as a helper and support. From them the race of mankind has sprung. You said, 'It is not good that the man should be alone; let us make a helper for him like himself.' And now, 'O Lord, I am not taking this sister of mine because of lust, but with sincerity. Grant that I may find mercy and may grow old together with her.' And they both said, 'Amen, Amen.' Then they both went to sleep for the night (Tob 8:5-9)" (ibid., p. 24).

[6]Ibid., p. 36.

[7]1 Corinthians 7:32-37.

[8]And even when I was not engaged in those things, my mind was. Eventually, as popular author Merlin Carothers noted, What was on my mind was manifested in my life (Merlin Carothers, *What's On Your Mind?* [Escondido: Calif.: Merlin Carothers Publishing, 1984], pp. 40-41). Estévez writes about the permissive culture in which I had placed myself (and of which my parents certainly would not have approved!), "Permissiveness, which is the result of a society, having no clear and objective standards with which to evaluate conduct, tends to support the impression that a type of conduct is automatically respectable and acceptable as long as the majority behave that way. 'Pluralism' now enters into play, conceived of not only as an affirmation of differences, but also as an impediment to the pronouncement of moral judgments and as a hindrance to the claim that the truth actually exists, and not just 'my' truth and 'your' truth" (Estévez, *Male and Female,* p. 156).

[9]1 John 1:9.

[10]Mother Teresa, *A Gift for God* (San Francisco: HarperSanFrancisco, 1996), pp. 37-38.

[11]Brother Angelo Devananda (Scolozzi), *Contemplative in the Heart of the World* (New York: Fount, 1985), p. 76.

Chapter 12: Small Things with Great Love

[1]EWTN Global Catholic Network, "The Anima Christi" <www.ewtn.com/devotionals/prayers/anima2.htm>.

[2] Brother Lawrence of the Resurrection, *The Practice of the Presence of God* (New York: Image Books, 1977), p. 29.

Chapter 13: Prayer Is Our First Work

[1]José Luis González-Balado, ed., *Loving Jesus* (Ann Arbor, Mich.: Servant, 1991), p. 36.

[2]C. Peter Wagner and Pablo A. Deiros, eds., *The Rising Revival: What the Spirit Is Saying Through the Argentine Revival* (Ventura, Calif.: Gospel Light, 1998), pp. 171-84.

[3]See, for example, Ed Silvoso, *That None Should Perish* (Ventura, Calif.: Regal, 1994); El Silvoso, *Prayer Evangelism* (Ventura, Calif.: Regal, 2000); John Dawson, *Taking Our Cities for God* (Lake Mary, Fla.: Charisma House, 2001); George Otis, *Informed Intercession* (Ventura, Calif.: Renew Books, 1999); Peter

Wagner, *Prayer Shield* (Ventura, Calif.: Regal, 1992). Also see *Transformations I: A Documentary*, prod. George Otis Jr., 58 min., Sentinel Group, 1999, DVD; *Transformations II: The Glory Spreads*, prod. George Otis Jr., 58 min., Sentinel Group, 2001, DVD; and *Let the Sea Resound*, prod. George Otis Jr., 79 min., Sentinel Group, 2004, DVD.

Chapter 14: The Missionaries and Miracles

[1]Peter Wagner and Pablo Deiros, *The Rising Revival* (Ventura, Calif.: Gospel Light, 1998).

[2]Heidi Baker, *There Is Always Enough* (Tonbridge, U.K.: Sovereign World, 2003).

[3]C. S. Lewis, *Miracles* (New York: Collier Books, 1978), pp. 60-61.

[4]Charles Kraft, *Christianity with Power* (Ann Arbor, Mich.: Vine Books, 1989), pp. 4-5.

[5]Henri Nouwen, *The Wounded Healer* (New York: Image Books, 1979).

Chapter 15: If We Say We Have No Sin, the Truth Is Not in Us

[1]Jeremiah 17:9: "The heart is deceitful above all things, and desperately wicked: who can know it?" (KJV).

[2]Matthew 15:19: "For out of the heart come evil thoughts, murder, adultery, sexual immorality, theft, false witness, slander."

[3]G. K. Chesterton, *Orthodoxy* (London: John Land, 1909), p. 22.

[4]Ravi Zacharias, *Can Man Live Without God?* (Nashville: Word, 1994), pp. 138-39. The article he refers to is Hobart Mowrer, "Sin, the Lesser of Two Evils," *The American Psychologist* 15, (1960): 301-4.

[5]1 John 1:9: "If we confess our sins, he is faithful and just to forgive us our sins and to cleanse us from all unrighteousness."

[6]Mother Teresa and Angelo Scolozzi, *Total Surrender* (Ann Arbor, Mich.: Saint Anthony Messenger Press and Franciscan Communications, 1985), p. 37.

[7]David Aikman, *Great Souls* (Nashville: Word, 1998), p. 153.

[8]José Luis González-Balado, *Heart of Joy* (Ann Arbor, Mich.: Servant, 1987), p. 133.

[9]Scolozzi, *Total Surrender*, p. 113.

[10]Paul Vitz, *Psychology as Religion: The Cult of Self-Worship* (Grand Rapids: Eerdmans, 1998).

Chapter 16: Here God's Grace More Abounds

[1]See, for example, Psalms 9:9; 10:1-8; 103:6; 146:7; Isaiah 61:3.

[2]Charles Kraft with Christie Varney and Ellen Kearney, *Christianity with Power* (Ann Arbor, Mich.: Vine, 1989), p. 26; See also Charles Kraft, *I Give You Authority* (Grand Rapids: Chosen, 1997).

Chapter 17: Sometimes We Get Lost When We Look at Numbers

[1]Mother Teresa, *Words to Live By* (Notre Dame, Ind.: Ave Maria Press, 1983), p. 25.
[2]Malcolm Muggeridge, *Something Beautiful for God* (New York: Image Books, 1977), p. 22.
[3]Mother Teresa, *A Gift for God* (San Francisco: HarperSanFrancisco, 1996), pp. 42, 45.
[4]Ann and Jeanette Petrie, *Mother Teresa* (Canada: Petrie Productions, 1986).
[5]Muggeridge, *Something Beautiful for God*, pp. 90-91.
[6]John 2:23-25.
[7]Mother Teresa, *Gift for God*, p. 44.

Chapter 18: Don't Give In to Discouragement

[1]Mother Teresa, *A Gift for God* (San Francisco: HarperSanFrancisco, 1996), p. 40.
[2] Mother Teresa and Angelo Scolozzi, *Total Surrender* (Ann Arbor, Mich.: Saint Anthony Messenger Press and Franciscan Communications, 1985), p. 119.
[3]Malcolm Muggeridge, *Something Beautiful for God* (New York: Image Books, 1977), p. 22.
[4]Matthew 6:34.
[5]Theophan the Recluse, *The Spiritual Life* (Platina, Calif.: St. Herman of Alaska Brotherhood, 1995), pp. 87, 93.
[6]Ibid., p. 94.
[7]Thomas Merton, *No Man Is an Island* (San Diego: Harvest, 1983), p. 169.
[8]James Talley, ed., *Jesus, The Living Bread* (Plainfield, N.J.: Logos International, 1976), p. 41.

Chapter 19: Mother Teresa's Dark Night of the Spirit

[1]Brian Kolodiejchuk, *Mother Teresa, Come Be My Light: The Private Writings of the "Saint of Calcutta"* (New York: Doubleday, 2007).
[2]Those in religious life have one or more people (generally also superiors) who help guide them in their spiritual life. They confess their struggles and failures to these confessors, and to God in their presence. As James says, "Con-

fess your sins to one another" (James 5:16).

[3]Ibid., p. 297.

[4]LaVonne Neff, ed., *A Life for God: The Mother Teresa Reader* (Ann Arbor, Mich.: Servant, 1995), p. 140.

[5]Galatians 4:19.

[6]Kolodiejchuk, *Come Be My Light*, p. 187.

[7]Ibid., p. 211.

[8]1 Corinthians 2:15-16: "The spiritual person judges all things, but is himself to be judged by no one. 'For who has understood the mind of the Lord so as to instruct him?' But we have the mind of Christ."

[9]John of the Cross, *The Collected Works of St. John of the Cross* (Washington, D.C.: Institute of Carmelite Studies, 1991), pp. 383-84.

[10]Angelo D. Scolozzi, *Thirsting for God: A Yearbook of Prayers and Meditations* (Ann Arbor, Mich.: Saint Anthony Messenger Press and Franciscan Communications, 2000), p. 132.

[11]*Agape* refers to the general affection of people for one another, such as in Jesus' commandment to love one another. *Eros* is romantic love, while *philia* represents the love of friendship.

[12]St. Francis de Sales, *Treatise on the Love of God* (Rockford, Ill.: Tan Books, 1997), p. 30.

[13]José Luis González-Balado and Mother Teresa, *Mother Teresa: In My Own Words* (New York: Gramercy Books, 1997), p. 31.

[14]Kolodiejchuk, *Come Be My Light*, p. 185.

[15]Ibid.

[16]Ibid., p. 237.

[17]Brother Angelo Devananda (Scolozzi), *Contemplative in the Heart of the World* (New York: Fount, 1985), p. 21.

[18]Kolodiejchuk, *Come Be My Light*, p. 141.

[19]Colossians 1:24.

[20]Mother Teresa, *A Gift for God* (San Francisco: HarperSanFrancisco, 1996), p. 89.

[21]1 Peter 4:19.

[22]Kolodiejchuk, *Come Be My Light*, p. 208.

[23]Joy Dawson, *Forever Ruined for the Ordinary* (Seattle: YWAM Publishing, 2001).

[24]Gerald May, *The Dark Night of the Soul* (San Francisco: HarperSanFrancisco, 2005).

[25]Devananda (Scolozzi), *Contemplative in the Heart of the World*, p. 21.

[26]Isaiah 53:12: "Therefore I will divide him a portion with the many, / and he shall divide the spoil with the strong, / because he poured out his soul to death / and was numbered with the transgressors; / yet he bore the sin of many, / and makes intercession for the transgressors."

Chapter 20: The Humor of Mother Teresa
[1]Ann and Jeanette Petrie, *Mother Teresa* (Canada: Petrie Productions, 1986).
[2]Father Angelo Scolozzi, personal communication, Pecos Benedictine Monastery, August 11, 2003.
[3]Edward Le Joly, *Mother Teresa: A Woman in Love* (Notre Dame, Ind.: Ave Maria Press, 1993), p. 58.
[4]Ibid., p. 69.
[5]Ibid., pp. 75-76
[6]Brother Angelo Devananda (Scolozzi), *Contemplative in the Heart of the World* (New York: Fount, 1985), p. 116.
[7]James Talley, ed., *Jesus, The Living Bread* (Plainfield, N.J.: Logos International, 1976), p. 43.

Chapter 21: Spreading the Fragrance of Christ
[1]A popular work of Joyce Meyer is her book *Battlefield of the Mind* (Tulsa, Okla.: Harrison, 1995).

Chapter 22. It Matters Not, He Is Forgiven
[1]Christopher Hitchens, *The Missionary Position* (New Dehli: Indus/HarperCollins, 1995). This author has now written an atheist book, *God Is Not Great,* and suggested in *Newsweek* magazine, August 20, 2007, that Mother's "dark night of the soul" indicated that she did not believe there was a God.
[2]Ed Silvoso, *That None Should Perish* (Ventura, Calif.: Regal, 1994).
[3]Pastor Che Ahn of Harvest Rock Church in Pasadena, Calif.
[4]R. T. Kendall, *Total Forgiveness* (Lake Mary, Fla.: Charisma House, 2002).
[5]José Luis González-Balado, *One Heart Full of Love* (Ann Arbor, Mich.: Servant, 1988), p. 5.
[6]Ibid., p. 37.
[7]Mother Teresa, *A Gift for God* (San Francisco: HarperSanFrancisco, 1996), pp. 54-55, 58-59.
[8]Ann and Jeanette Petrie, *Mother Teresa* (Canada: Petrie Productions, 1986).
[9]Lewis Smedes, *Forgive and Forget* (New York: Pocket, 1984).

[10]Father Angelo Scolozzi, personal communication, Beaumont, Tex., January 2008.

[11]Brian Kolodiejchuk, *Mother Teresa, Come Be My Light: The Private Writings of the "Saint of Calcutta"* (New York: Doubleday, 2007), p. 323.

[12]Mother Teresa, *Gift for God*, pp. 34-35.

[13]Angelo D. Scolozzi, *Thirsting for God: A Yearbook of Prayers and Meditations* (Ann Arbor, Mich.: Saint Anthony Messenger Press and Franciscan Communications, 2000), p. 56.

Chapter 23: Fighting Abortion with Adoption

[1]Minnesota Citizens Concerned for Life (February 13, 2008) <www.mccl.org/abortion_statistics.htm>.

[2]Nell Noddings, *Caring: A Feminine Approach to Ethics and Moral Education* (Berkeley: University of California Press, 1984), p. 87.

[3]Hebrews 4:12: "For the word of God is living and active, sharper than any two-edged sword, piercing to the division of soul and of spirit, of joints and of marrow, and discerning the thoughts and intentions of the heart."

[4]William Clinton, "Remarks at the National Prayer Breakfast," February 7, 1994. Peggy Noonan wrote, "She spoke with a complete indifference to the conventions of speech. . . . She softened nothing. . . . She could do this, of course, because she had a natural and unknown authority. She has the standing of a saint" (Peggy Noonan, "Still, Small Voice," *Crisis Magazine*, February 1, 1998 <www.peggynoonan.com/article.php?article=295>).

[5]Lush Gjergji, *Mother Teresa: To Live, to Love, to Witness, Her Spiritual Way* (New York: New City, 1998), pp. 31-32.

Chapter 24: Give Until It Hurts

[1]Matthew 6:3-4.

[2]All About Jewish Charity and Justice (March 4, 2008) <www.tzedaka.org>.

[3]LaVonne Neff, *A Life for God: The Mother Teresa Reader* (Ann Arbor, Mich.: Servant, 1995), p. 82.

[4]Susan Conroy, *Mother Teresa: Lessons of Love and Secrets of Sanctity* (Huntington, Ind.: Our Sunday Visitor Publishing, 2003), p. 208.

Chapter 25: Revolutionaries for Love

[1]José Luis González-Balado, *Heart of Joy* (Ann Arbor, Mich.: Servant, 1987), p. 41.

[2]Malcolm Muggeridge, *Something Beautiful for God* (New York: Image Books, 1977), p. 49.

[3]Ibid., p. 87.

[4]José Luis González-Balado, *One Heart Full of Love* (Ann Arbor, Mich.: Servant, 1988), p. 8.

[5]Studs Terkel, *Working* (New York: Pantheon, 1984), p. xxiv.

[6]Martin Luther King Jr., Clayborne Carson and Peter Halloran, eds., *A Knock at Midnight: Inspiration from the Great Sermons of Reverend Martin Luther King, Jr.* (New York: Grand Central Publishing, 1998), p. 126.

[7]Angelo D. Scolozzi, *Thirsting for God: A Yearbook of Prayers and Meditations* (Ann Arbor, Mich.: Saint Anthony Messenger Press and Franciscan Communications, 2000), p. 89.

[8]Scott Bessenecker, *The New Friars* (Downers Grove, Ill.: InterVarsity Press, 2006). Also see Albert Holtz, *Downtown Monks* (Notre Dame, Ind.: Ave Maria Press, 2000); Colleen Carroll, *The New Faithful: Why Young Adults are Embracing Christian Orthodoxy* (Chicago: Loyola Press, 2002); David Ruis, *The Justice God Is Seeking* (Ventura, Calif.: Regal, 2006); Mark Labberton, *The Dangerous Act of Worship: Living God's Call to Justice* (Downers Grove, Ill.: InterVarsity Press, 2007). Other recent works on the call to justice include Michael Emerson and Christian Smith, *Divided by Faith* (Oxford: Oxford University Press, 2000); Gary Haugen, *Good News About Injustice* (Downers Grove, Ill.: InterVarsity Press, 1999); N. T. Wright, *Evil and the Justice of God* (Downers Grove, Ill.: InterVarsity Press, 2006); Andy Freeman and Peter Greig, *Punk Monk* (Ventura, Calif.: Regal, 2007); Dick Staub, *The Culturally Savvy Christian* (San Francisco: Jossey-Bass, 2007).

[9]Mary Fairchild, "Christianity Today—General Statistics and Facts of Christianity," About.com <christianity.about.com/od/denominations/p/christianity-today.htm>.

[10]Mother Teresa, *A Gift for God* (San Francisco: HarperSanFrancisco, 1996), p. 20.

Chapter 26: Mother Teresa and the Body of Christ

[1]Brian Kolodiejchuk, *Mother Teresa, Come Be My Light: The Private Writings of the "Saint of Calcutta"* (New York: Doubleday, 2007), p. 76.

[2]Brother Angelo Devananda (Scolozzi), *Contemplative in the Heart of the World* (New York: Fount, 1985), p. 87.

[3]Galatians 3:28: "There is neither Jew nor Greek, there is neither slave nor free, there is no male and female, for you are all one in Christ Jesus." Colossians 3:11: "Here there is not Greek and Jew, circumcised and uncircumcised, barbarian, Scythian, slave, free; but Christ is all, and in all."

[4]2 Corinthians 12:9-10: "But he said to me, 'My grace is sufficient for you, for my power is made perfect in weakness.' Therefore I will boast all the more gladly of my weaknesses, so that the power of Christ may rest upon me. For the sake of Christ, then, I am content with weaknesses, insults, hardships, persecutions, and calamities. For when I am weak, then I am strong."

[5]Michael Collopy, *Works of Love are Works of Peace* (San Francisco: Ignatius Press, 1996).

[6]Gandhi, *An Autobiography: The Story of My Experiments with Truth* (Boston: Beacon, 1993), p. 68.

[7]Martin Luther King Jr., Clayborne Carson and Peter Halloran, eds., *A Knock at Midnight: Inspiration from the Great Sermons of Reverend Martin Luther King, Jr.* (New York: Grand Central Publishing, 1998), p. 208.

[8]1 Corinthians 12:12-31: "For just as the body is one and has many members, and all the members of the body, though many, are one body, so it is with Christ. For in one Spirit we were all baptized into one body—Jews or Greeks, slaves or free—and all were made to drink of one Spirit. For the body does not consist of one member but of many. If the foot should say, 'Because I am not a hand, I do not belong to the body,' that would not make it any less a part of the body. And if the ear should say, 'Because I am not an eye, I do not belong to the body,' that would not make it any less a part of the body. If the whole body were an eye, where would be the sense of hearing? If the whole body were an ear, where would be the sense of smell? But as it is, God arranged the members in the body, each one of them, as he chose. If all were a single member, where would the body be? As it is, there are many parts, yet one body. The eye cannot say to the hand, 'I have no need of you,' nor again the head to the feet, 'I have no need of you.' On the contrary, the parts of the body that seem to be weaker are indispensable, and on those parts of the body that we think less honorable we bestow the greater honor, and our unpresentable parts are treated with greater modesty, which our more presentable parts do not require. But God has so composed the body, giving greater honor to the part that lacked it, that there may be no division in the body, but that the members may have the same care for one another. If one member suffers, all suffer together; if one member is honored, all rejoice together. Now you are the body of Christ and individu- ally members of it. And God has appointed in the church first apostles, second prophets, third teachers, then miracles, then gifts of healing, helping, admin- istrating, and various kinds of tongues. Are all apostles? Are all prophets? Are all teachers? Do all work miracles? Do all possess gifts of healing? Do all speak

with tongues? Do all interpret? But earnestly desire the higher gifts."
[9]Philip Jenkins, *The Next Christendom* (Oxford: Oxford University Press, 2002); Philip Jenkins, *God's Continent: Christianity, Islam and Europe's Religion Crisis* (Oxford: Oxford University Press, 2007); Peter Wagner, *Changing Church* (Ventura, Calif.: Regal Books); John Armstrong, *True Revival* (Eugene, Ore.: Harvest House, 2001); Peter Wagner, *Churchquake* (Ventura, Calif.: Regal, 2000); Francis McNutt, *The Healing Reawakening* (Grand Rapids: Chosen, 2005); John and Paula Sandford, *Prophets, Healers and the Emerging Church* (Shippensburg, Penn.: Destiny Image, 2003).

Chapter 27: The Uniqueness of Christ
[1]Psalm 37:4: "Delight yourself in the LORD, / and he will give you the desires of your heart."
[2]Mark 16:15.
[3]Craig Smith, *Whiteman's Gospel* (Winnepeg, Man.: Indian Life Ministries, 1997); Richard Twiss and John Dawson, *One Church, Many Tribes* (Ventura, Calif.: Regal, 2000); John Dawson, *Taking our Cities for God* (Lake Mary, Fla.: Charisma House, 1990); Vincent Donovan, *Christianity Rediscovered* (New York: Orbis, 1997); Lesslie Newbigin, *Foolishness to the Greeks: The Gospel and Western Culture* (Grand Rapids: Eerdmans, 1986); Charles Kraft, *Christianity and Power* (Ann Arbor, Mich.: Vine, 1989).
[4]Newbigin, *Foolishness to the Greeks*, p. 4.
[5]I use the term *Judeo-Christian* because the principles of Christianity include and build on the principles of Judaism.
[6]Philip Jenkins, *The Next Christendom: The Coming of Global Christianity* (Oxford: Oxford University Press, 2002).
[7]C. Peter Wagner and Pablo A. Deiros, eds., *The Rising Revival: What the Spirit Is Saying Through the Argentine Revival* (Ventura, Calif.: Gospel Light, 1998).
[8]Brian Kolodiejchuk, *Mother Teresa, Come Be My Light: The Private Writings of the "Saint of Calcutta"* (New York: Doubleday, 2007), p. 97.

Chapter 28: Leaving Calcutta
[1]Sofia Cavaletti, *The Religious Potential of the Child* (Chicago: Liturgy Training Publications, 1992).
[2]Daniel Stramara, *Driven by the Spirit: The Life of Saint Francis of Rome* (Pecos, N.M.: Dove, 1992).
[3]Jean Vanier, *An Arch for the Poor* (Toronto: Novalis, 1995); Jean Vanier, *Commu-*

nity and Growth (New York: Paulist Press, 1989); Henri Nouwen, *The Wounded Healer* (New York: Image Books, 1979).
[4]Psalm 127:1-2: "Unless the LORD builds the house, those who build it labor in vain. Unless the LORD watches over the city, the watchman stays awake in vain. It is in vain that you rise up early and go late to rest, eating the bread of anxious toil; for he gives to his beloved sleep."

Chapter 29: Finding Calcutta
[1]C. J. De Catanzaro, *Symeon, the New Theologian: The Discourses* (New York: Paulist Press, 1980), p. 83. Thanks to Warren of Eighth Day Bookstore in Kansas for the recommendation.

Chapter 30: My Thoughts Are Not Your Thoughts
[1]John 1:1-3, 14.
[2]Hebrews 1:3 NRSV.
[3]Colossians 1:11-17.
[4]Dallas Willard, *The Divine Conspiracy* (San Francisco: HarperSanFrancisco, 1998), p. 95.
[5]Matthew 13:25.
[6]Many excellent university faculty members have written boldly about these issues; among them are George Marsden, Dallas Willard, Charles Malik, Kelly Monroe, John Henry Newman, Mark Noll, James Burtchaell and John Sommerville. Many more faculty work in their own particular fields to incorporate Christian principles. The meeting places include meetings sponsored by InterVarsity, Campus Crusade, Catholic Scholars, Veritas, C. S. Lewis Foundation, International Institute for Christian Studies and *Touchstone* magazine.
[7]Romans 12:1-2: "I appeal to you therefore, brothers, by the mercies of God, to present your bodies as a living sacrifice, holy and acceptable to God, which is your spiritual worship. Do not be conformed to this world, but be transformed by the renewal of your mind, that by testing you may discern what is the will of God, what is good and acceptable and perfect."
[8]See the discussion of the transformations of the Harvard seal in Kelly Monroe Kullberg, *Finding God at Harvard* (Downers Grove, Ill.: IVP Books, 2007); Julie Reuben, *The Making of the Modern University: Intellectual Transformation and the Marginalization of Morality* (Chicago: University of Chicago Press, 1996).
[9]Books that help in this area include Charles Colson and Nancy Pearcey, *How Now Shall We Live?* (Wheaton, Ill.: Tyndale, 1999); James W. Sire, *Habits of*

the Mind (Downers Grove, Ill.: InterVarsity Press, 2000); Art Lindsley, *True Truth* (Downers Grove, Ill.: InterVarsity Press, 2004); David Marshall, *The Truth Behind the New Atheism* (Eugene, Ore.: Harvest House, 2007); Timothy Keller, *The Reason for God* (New York: Dutton, 2008); Alister McGrath, *Bridge-Building* (Leicester, U.K.: Inter-Varsity Press, 1992); David Dockery and Gregory Thornbury, *Shaping a Christian Worldview* (Nashville: Broadman and Holman, 2002); Gene Veith, *Postmodern Times* (Wheaton, Ill.: Crossway, 1994); Dick Staub, *The Culturally Savvy Christian* (San Francisco: Jossey-Bass, 2007).

[10]Colson and Pearcey, *How Now Shall We Live?* p. 22.

[11]Richard John Neuhaus, *The Best of the Public Square: Book Two* (Grand Rapids: Eerdmans, 2001), p. 101.

[12]Todd Lake, "My Search for the Historical Jesus," in Kelly Monroe Kullberg, *Finding God at Harvard* (Downers Grove, Ill.: IVP Books, 2007), p. 43.

[13]John 8:31-34: "So Jesus said to the Jews who had believed in him, 'If you abide in my word, you are truly my disciples, and you will know the truth, and the truth will set you free.' They answered him, 'We are offspring of Abraham and have never been enslaved to anyone. How is it that you say, "You will become free"?' Jesus answered them, 'Truly, truly, I say to you, everyone who commits sin is a slave to sin.'"

Epilogue: Fall More in Love with Jesus Every Day

[1]Luke 6:32.

[2]Matthew 22:37-39.

[3]José Luis González-Balado, *Heart of Joy* (Ann Arbor, Mich.: Servant, 1987), p. 119.

Appendix A: A Brief History of the University and Dominant Worldviews

[1]Jaroslav Pelikan, *Jesus Through the Centuries* (New Haven, Conn.: Yale University Press, 1985), p. 1.

[2]William Jeynes, *American Educational History: School, Society and the Common Good* (Thousand Oaks, Calif.: Sage, 2007).

[3]James Burtchaell, *The Dying of the Light: The Disengagement of Colleges and Universities from their Christian Churches* (Grand Rapids: Eerdmans, 1998).

[4]William Buckley, *God and Man at Yale* (Washington, D.C.: Regnery, 1951). See also John Henry Newman, *The Idea of the University* (Notre Dame, Ind.: University of Notre Dame Press, 1982); Charles Malik, *A Christian Critique of the University* (Waterloo, Ont.: North Waterloo Academic Press, 1987);

George Marsden, *The Soul of the American University* (Oxford: Oxford University Press, 1994); James Burtchaell, *The Dying of the Light* (Grand Rapids: Eerdmans, 1998); Philip Gleason, *Contending with Modernity: Catholic Higher Education in the Twentieth Century* (Oxford: Oxford University Press, 1995); C. John Sommerville, *The Decline of the Secular University* (Oxford: Oxford Unviersity Press, 2006); Kelly Monroe Kullberg, *Finding God at Harvard* (Downers Grove, Ill.: IVP Books, 2007); Naomi Schaefer Riley, *God on the Quad* (New York: St. Martin's Press, 2005).

[5]George Marsden, *The Outrageous Idea of Christian Scholarship* (Oxford: Oxford University Press, 1994).

[6]Kathy Bassard, "Scripture Meditation: How Shall We Sing the Lord's Song in a Foreign Land? (aka Grab Your Harp)" (Berkeley, Calif.: C. S. Lewis Conference on Academic Freedom, October 11, 2003).

[7]This is not unlike what Paul encountered when he first visited Athens after his conversion. He was called a babbler and a preacher of foreign deities. Acts 17:16-21: "Now while Paul was waiting for them at Athens, his spirit was provoked within him as he saw that the city was full of idols. So he reasoned in the synagogue with the Jews and the devout persons, and in the marketplace every day with those who happened to be there. Some of the Epicurean and Stoic philosophers also conversed with him. And some said, 'What does this babbler wish to say?' Others said, 'He seems to be a preacher of foreign divinities'—because he was preaching Jesus and the resurrection. And they took him and brought him to the Areopagus, saying, 'May we know what this new teaching is that you are presenting? For you bring some strange things to our ears. We wish to know therefore what these things mean.' Now all the Athenians and the foreigners who lived there would spend their time in nothing except telling or hearing something new."

[8]Dinesh D'Souza, *What's So Great About Christianity* (Washington, D.C.: Regnery, 2007); Rodney Stark, *For the Glory of God* (Princeton, N.J.: Princeton University Press, 2003); Rodney Stark, *One True God* (Princeton, N.J.: Princeton University Press, 2001); Jonathan Hill, *What Has Christianity Ever Done for Us?* (Downers Grove, Ill.: InterVarsity Press, 2005); Dick Staub, *The Culturally Savvy Christian* (San Francisco: Jossey-Bass, 2007).

[9]Paul Vitz, *Censorship: Evidence of Bias in Our Children's Textbooks* (Ann Arbor, Mich.: Servant, 1986).

[10]Martin Luther King Jr., Clayborne Carson and Peter Halloran, eds., *A Knock at Midnight: Inspiration from the Great Sermons of Reverend Martin Luther King, Jr.*

(New York: Grand Central Publishing, 1998).

[11]Paul Vitz, *Psychology as Religion: The Cult of Self-Worship* (Grand Rapids, Mich.: Eerdmans, 1998).

[12]Isaiah 61:3: "to grant to those who mourn in Zion— / to give them a beautiful headdress instead of ashes, / the oil of gladness instead of mourning, / the garment of praise instead of a faint spirit; / that they may be called oaks of righteousness, / the planting of the LORD, that he may be glorified."

[13]Proverbs 13:11: "Wealth gained hastily will dwindle, / but whoever gathers little by little will increase it"; Proverbs 13:22: "A good man leaves an inheritance to his children's children, / but the sinner's wealth is laid up for the righteous."

[14]2 Peter 1:5-7: "For this very reason, make every effort to supplement your faith with virtue, and virtue with knowledge, and knowledge with self-control, and self-control with steadfastness, and steadfastness with godliness, and godliness with brotherly affection, and brotherly affection with love."

[15]Julie Reuben, *The Making of the Modern University: Intellectual Transformation and the Marginalization of Morality* (Chicago: University of Chicago Press, 1996).

[16]James Burtchaell, "All the Essential Truths about Higher Education," *First Things*, October 1998.

[17]Dallas Willard, *Hearing God: Developing a Conversational Relationship with God* (Downers Grove, Ill.: InterVarsity Press, 1999), pp. 218 19.

[18]Francis Collins, *The Language of God: A Scientist Presents Evidence for Belief* (New York: Free Press, 2006), pp. 228-29.

[19]Lesslie Newbigin, *Foolishness to the Greeks: The Gospel and Western Culture* (Grand Rapids: Eerdmans, 1986), pp. 22, 54.

[20]The new atheists' books include Richard Dawkins, *The God Delusion* (Boston: Houghton Mifflin, 2006); Daniel Dennett, *Breaking the Spell* (New York: Penguin Books, 2006); Sam Harris, *Letter to a Christian Nation* (New York: Knopf, 2007); Christopher Hitchens, *God Is Not Great* (New York: Twelve, 2007).

Some books countering these views include Francis S. Collins, *The Language of God* (New York: Free Press, 2006); Alister McGrath and Joanna Collicutt McGrath, *The Dawkins Delusion?* (Downers Grove, Ill.: IVP Books, 2007); Dinesh D'Souza, *What's So Great About Christianity?* (Washington, D.C.: Regnery, 2007); David Marshall, *The Truth Behind the New Atheism* (Eugene, Ore.: Harvest House, 2007); Timothy Keller, *The Reason for God* (New York: Dutton, 2008).

[21]Peter Kreeft, ed., *A Summa of the Summa* (San Francisco: Ignatius Press, 1990).

[22]References for scientists who question the theory of evolution across species: Michael Behe, *Darwin's Black Box: The Biochemical Challenge to Evolution* (New York: Simon & Schuster, 1996); Phillip E. Johnson, *The Right Questions* (Downers Grove, Ill.: InterVarsity Press, 2002); Phillip E. Johnson, *Darwin on Trial* (Downers Grove, Ill.: InterVarsity Press, 1993); William Dembski, *The Design Revolution* (Downers Grove, Ill.: InterVarsity Press, 2004); William Dembski, *The Design Inference* (Cambridge: Cambridge University Press, 1998).

[23]References for scientists who hold to a theistic view of evolution include: Collins, *Language of God;* Darrel Falk, *Coming to Peace with Science* (Downers Grove, Ill.: InterVarsity Press, 2004); Kenneth Miller, *Finding Darwin's God* (New York: Harper Perennial, 2000); John Polkinghorne, *Exploring Reality: The Intertwining of Science and Religion* (New Haven, Conn.: Yale University Press, 2005).

[24]Francis Collins, *Language of God,* pp. 233-34.

[25]James Emery White, "Science and Religion: No Place for God," *Serious Times* 4, no. 2 (March 4, 2008), available at <www.seriustimes.com/blog.asp?ID=53>. See also Ben Stein's movie *Expelled.*

[26]Antony Flew, *A Dictionary of Philosophy* (New York: St. Martin's, 1984), p. 153.

[27]Paul Kurtz, *Council for Secular Humanism* (March 4, 2008) <www.secular humanism.org/index.php?page=what&section=main>.

[28]Peter Singer, *Practical Ethics* (Cambridge: Cambridge University Press, 1993). See also Peter Singer, *In Defense of Animals: The Second Wave* (Oxford: Blackwell, 2006); *Rethinking Life and Death* (Melbourne, Australia: Text, 1995). For a critique, see Gordon Preece, *Rethinking Peter Singer: A Christian Critique* (Downers Grove, Ill.: InterVarsity Press, 2002).

[29]*Diagnostic and Statistical Manual of Mental Disorders, TR,* 4th ed. (Washington, D.C.: American Psychiatric Association, 1987).

[30]C. S. Lewis, *Mere Christianity* (New York: Simon & Schuster, 1980), p. 56.

[31]W. Robert Connor, "The Right Time and Place for Big Questions," *The Chronicle of Higher Education* 52, no. 40 (July 9, 2006): B8.

[32]James Herrick, *The Making of the New Spirituality: The Eclipse of the Western Religious Tradition* (Downers Grove, Ill.: InterVarsity Press, 2003).

[33]John 3:3: "Jesus answered him, 'Truly, truly, I say to you, unless one is born again he cannot see the kingdom of God.' "

[34]Ephesians 6:12: "For we do not wrestle against flesh and blood, but against principalities, against powers, against the rulers of the darkness of this age, against spiritual hosts of wickedness in the heavenly places" (NKJV).

[35]Philip Jenkins, "Europe's Christian Comeback," *Foreign Policy* (June 2007). Available at <www.foreignpolicy.com/story/cms.php?story_id=3881>.

Appendix B: Toward a Twenty-First-Century University

[1]Stanley Fish, "One University, Under God?" *The Chronicle of Higher Education* 51, no. 18 (January 7, 2005): C1.

[2]C. John Sommerville, *The Decline of the Secular University* (Oxford: Oxford University Press, 2006).

[3]Edward Kaplan, "Jewish renewal in pre-nazi Berlin: Abraham Heschel interprets William James" (Association for Religion and Intellectual Life, 2003) <findarticles.com/p/articles/mi_m2096/is_3_53/ai_112212960>.

[4]William Craig, *On Being a Christian Academic* (Addison, Tex.: Lewis and Stanley, 2004).

[5]James W. Sire, *The Universe Next Door* (Downers Grove, Ill.: InterVarsity Press, 1997), p. 1. Sire's list of worldviews includes Christian theism, deism, naturalism, nihilism, existentialism, Eastern pantheistic monism, the New Age and postmodernism.

[6]Augustine, *Expositions of the Psalms,* quoted in George Howie, *Educational Theory and Practice in St. Augustine* (London: Routledge and Kegan Paul, 1969), p. 53.

[7]Mark Noll, *The Scandal of the Evangelical Mind* (Grand Rapids: Eerdmans, 1994).

For Further Reflection

Resources to begin: Video titled *Mother Teresa* by Ann and Jeanette Petrie, narrated by Richard Attenborough (available from Ignatius Press); Malcolm Muggeridge's *Something Beautiful for God*; Father Angelo Scolozzi's *Total Surrender* or *Thirsting for God*; Father Brian Kolodiejchuk's *Come Be My Light* or other books about Mother Teresa listed in the notes.

Introduction: Telling the Truth About Mother Teresa

1. Read and reflect on Jeremiah 29:11-14; Ephesians 1:15-21; 4:1-7; and Philippians 1:6.

2. How have you searched for or found your Calcutta? What experiences have you had that may be or were significant in revealing your calling?

3. Select a biblical character and trace their journey to their destiny, their Calcutta.

4. Describe an experience where you knew something that you could not share with other people, because you knew their worldviews would not allow them to comprehend it.

5. What were the circumstances that surrounded your own conversion?

Chapter 1: Getting There

1. Read and reflect on Psalm 37:3-6; Psalm 127; and Proverbs 16:1-3.

2. Describe a time when you were so surrounded by grace, favor and guidance that you knew it was a special time of anointing from God.

3. Consider any of the disciples' moments of shaky trust. How do you identify with them?

4. Describe the struggles you have to fully trust in God and ways you have grown to trust God more.

5. Contemplate an area of your life that still needs to be relinquished to God's guidance. Pray for God to help you relinquish this.

Chapter 2: A Day in the Life of a Missionary of Charity

1. Read and reflect on Proverbs 3:5-10.

2. Think over a typical day in your life. Where do you have opportunities to do something beautiful for God? Who might most benefit from your fulfilling those opportunities?

3. In the Bible, there are ah-ha moments for many of God's people. Describe one that is meaningful to you.

4. Sometimes we have to give up particular parts of our day that draw us away from God rather than closer to him. Are there any parts of your day that need to be transformed?

5. What opportunities, no matter how small, might you take advantage of tomorrow to do something beautiful for God?

Chapter 3: A Pencil in God's Hand

1. Read and reflect on Philippians 2:1-11 and Colossians 1:29.

2. Describe a time when you knew it was God working through you for the good of others.

3. Describe the characteristics of a Bible character who said yes to God, and then describe one who said no. Reflect on these in your own life.

4. Read Matthew 1:26-38, 46-55 and reflect on the humility of Mary.

5. Imagine you are that person pulling the ricksha who comes to the door of the Missionaries. What would be your feelings, thoughts, hopes and fears?

Chapter 4: Whatever You Did for the Least of These, You Did for Me

1. Read and reflect on Matthew 25:31-46.

2. What are examples of Jesus serving humanity as he walked the Earth?

3. How do you serve other people? In what ways does your church serve those outside it?

4. Who are "the least of these" in your life that you could refresh, clothe, visit?

5. When are you "the least of these"?

Chapter 5: The Church as Flawed and Finite

1. Read and reflect on Romans 2:1-5; 5—8; and Ephesians 2:6.

2. For what reasons did Jesus criticize the religious leaders of the day?

3. Do we excuse the church too easily or critique it too harshly? Why do you think that is?

4. What failings of your own are most difficult for you to forgive or excuse in others?

5. What finite thing do you struggle most to overcome? How can the infinite overcome the finite?

Chapter 6: Do All Things Without Complaining or Disputing

1. Read and reflect on Philippians 2:14-18.

2. Describe moments when the spirits of criticism, anger and complaint in your own life have left negative consequences.

3. Consider the Mary and Martha story (Luke 10:38-42) in light of the issues in this chapter.

4. What would be left unspoken in your workplace or home if you spoke only "when necessary in order to get the work done"? How would your workplace or home be changed?

5. Read and discuss the power of the tongue in Psalm 50:19-21 and James 1:26.

Chapter 7: It All Belongs to God

1. Read and reflect on Psalms 37 and 50:7-15.

2. Have you ever tried to control a situation that would have been resolved more easily if left alone?

3. What biblical characters took situations into their own hands, to their detriment?

4. Contemplate the consequences of worry and fretting in your own life, and ways to counteract these.

5. What opportunities do you have to be more generous?

Chapter 8: There Is Always Enough

1. Read and reflect on Matthew 6:25-34. If possible, read the book or watch the video by Heidi and Rolland Baker, *There's Always Enough* or the video *Viva Christo Rey.*

2. How do our riches keep us poor in our relationship with God?

3. What one thing of comfort and value would you be willing to give up to give its value to the poor?

4. How do you live from a belief that resources are either plentiful or scarce?

5. Describe instances when you have seen God's divine providence.

Chapter 9: The Vow of Poverty and Service to the Poor

1. Read and reflect on Isaiah 58.

2. Who are the poorest of the poor in your life?

3. Reflect on any experiences you have had serving the poor—materially or spiritually.

4. Can you help the disadvantaged without being disadvantaged? Are there biblical examples?

5. In what ways are you the poorest of the poor?

Chapter 10: The Vow of Obedience

1. Read and reflect on 1 Samuel 15; Titus 3:1-7; and Hebrews 13:17.

2. Discuss the ways your culture encourages disobedience. How might you counter this?

3. What did obedience look like in the lives of Jesus' disciples?

4. What does obedience look like in your own life?

5. Think of places in your own life where an increase in obedience is necessary. What might God be asking you to do?

Chapter 11: The Vow of Chastity

1. Read and reflect on 1 Corinthians 7.

2. Identify the ways that things in culture tempt us away from chastity with our bodies and our minds.

3. Look at biblical examples of being holy in marriage.

4. What might it mean to be chaste of heart? How can we move toward that kind of holiness?

5. Are impure thoughts sinful? Why or why not? Read Merlin Carothers's *What's on Your Mind?*

Chapter 12: Small Things with Great Love

1. Read and reflect on 1 Corinthians 13.

2. Describe instances of small things that others have done with great love for you or someone you know.

3. When did Jesus and the disciples do small things with great love as they passed through the countryside?

4. Is there a worldly attachment that causes you to miss doing small things with great love?

5. What are some ways you might do more small things with great love?

Chapter 13: Prayer Is Our First Work

1. Read and reflect on Romans 8:26-27; 12:12; Philippians 4:5-7; Colossians 4:2; and 1 Thessalonians 5:16-18.

2. How do you think prayer works? Discuss times when prayer has changed things in your life or the lives of others.

3. Does the Lord's Prayer cover all possibilities of prayer?

4. Why do you think we sometimes feel one person's prayers are

more effective than others? Do you think they actually are?

5. Think of and share (or write down) the different ways you pray. See any of the Transformatins videos (prod. George Otis Jr.).

Chapter 14: The Missionaries and Miracles

1. Read and reflect on Jesus' miracles; for example, Matthew 9:22; Mark 5:34; 10:52; Luke 8:48; 17:19; 18:42; and Acts 14:9.

2. What relationship do you think faith has with miracles?

3. What can we learn from the miracles of Jesus recorded in Scripture?

4. Do you believe miracles still happen today? Share with one another any miracles you have seen or know about.

5. Discuss C. S. Lewis's definition of a miracle.

Chapter 15: If We Say We Have No Sin, the Truth Is Not in Us

1. Read and reflect on Isaiah 64:6 and 1 John 1.

2. Describe a time when you "got up and went to your Father."

3. What things does the world say are "acceptable" that, in "God's truth," are actually sinful?

4. How and when do you search your heart for unconfessed sin?

5. In what ways are the problems in the workplace or home like the problems in our hearts?

Chapter 16: Here God's Grace More Abounds

1. Read and reflect on Psalm 9:9; 10:18; 103:6; 146:7; and Isaiah 61:1-3.

2. Describe the ways Paul experienced the grace of God.

3. How has God's grace worked in your weakness?

4. In what ways might wealth and comfort hinder recognition of God's grace?

5. Where have you seen God's grace abound?

Chapter 17: Sometimes We Get Lost When We Look at Numbers

1. Read and reflect on Psalm 131.

2. In what ways have you been distracted by thinking too largely?

3. Consider Jesus' example of washing the feet of the disciples; what does this tell us about work?

4. What big dreams of social justice might be well served by many people doing small tasks?

5. Describe a time when less talk and more action was or is needed. What practical steps can you take to help the action get done?

Chapter 18: Don't Give In to Discouragement

1. Read and reflect on Judges 6—7, the story of Gideon.

2. Discuss Theophan's ideas of the discrepancy between progressive dreams and actions.

3. What things tempt you to discouragement? What do you do with feelings of despair?

4. Consider Acts 6:1-7 in light of these issues. How do you emotionally respond to what God does in this passage?

5. Describe times when you have worked by faith despite discouragement.

Chapter 19: Mother Teresa's Dark Night of the Spirit

1. Read and reflect on Colossians 1:24-26.

2. Reflect on times of darkness in your own spiritual life. What was the result?

3. Consider Peter walking on water in Matthew 14:22-32. Can faith and doubt coexist?

4. Reflect on times when you have suffered for believing in Christ. How did this affect you?

5. Discuss ways that our emotions or our rationalizing can draw us away from our calling. How can you stay on track?

Chapter 20: The Humor of Mother Teresa

1. Read Isaiah 61:1-4, and reflect on the role of praise and joy.

2. Are there instances of humor in the Bible?

3. Discuss times in your life when you laughed at what God was doing.

4. Who does smiling most affect: the one smiling or the one who receives the smile?

5. Since we are made in God's image, what is the purpose of our humor, joy, praise and dancing?

Chapter 21: Spreading the Fragrance of Christ

1. In what ways do you leave people better and happier?

2. What stories in Scripture most demonstrate people spreading the fragrance of Christ?

3. We often hear of the "big miracles" of Jesus; describe some instances of him spreading his fragrance to others.

4. Describe a person you know who most spreads the fragrance of Christ.

5. What are three ways you can spread the fragrance of Christ that you are not yet doing?

Chapter 22: It Matters Not, He Is Forgiven

1. Read and reflect on Matthew 6:1-14 and 18:15-34.

2. Reflect on times when unforgiveness had destructive consequences for you or someone you love. Have you ever been forgiven in a powerful way by another person? Discuss the process of reaching full forgiveness.

3. Read Romans 5:3-5, 8:18; 2 Corinthians 1:6-7; Philippians 3:7-15; 1 Peter 1:6-9; 2:19-20; and 4:12-13.

4. What do you think Paul means in Philippians 3:1-11, particularly about "sharing in the sufferings" of Christ?

5. When have you felt joy or purpose in the midst of suffering? Describe a time when suffering led you to an increase in holiness.

Chapter 23: Fighting Abortion with Adoption

1. Read and reflect on Psalm 51 and 1 John 1:9.

2. Reflect on things for which you have not fully rested in the forgiveness of God. How can you try to rest in his forgiveness and grace?

3. Is there any sin that is unforgivable?

4. Describe a time when, after confessing, God cleansed you even the of unholy desire.

5. How can pride be behind both too high self-esteem and too low self-esteem?

Chapter 24: Give Until It Hurts

1. Read and reflect on Isaiah 58 and Matthew 6:1-4.

2. Have you ever been disappointed when you gave sacrificially and it was not noticed?

3. Discuss the widow's offering in Luke 21:1-4.

4. Describe times when you have given to others at great cost.

5. Describe times when others have given to you even though it hurt them. How did you receive this?

Chapter 25: Revolutionaries for Love

1. Read and reflect on the love verses in Luke 6:32; John 13; and 1 Corinthians 13.

2. Describe some "revolutionaries for love" in the Bible.

3. How can you be a revolutionary for love in your own home or workplace?

4. Do you have a desire to be completely focused on expressing Christ's love? In what form do you feel the calling?

5. How could you be a part of a group who would become revolutionaries for love?

Chapter 26: Mother Teresa and the Body of Christ

1. Read and reflect on 1 Corinthians 12.

2. Describe others in the body of Christ who are different from you in particular ways.

3. How were Paul and Peter different in their callings in the body of Christ?

4. How would you describe the core beliefs of the "orthodox" body of Christ across denominations?

5. Describe yourself as a member of the body of Christ. If you are a molecule in his body, where might you be (the head, the heart, the blood, the hands)? What do you see as your function and how might you work with others to do that better?

Chapter 27: The Uniqueness of Christ

1. Read and reflect on Genesis 1:1-3; John 1; Colossians 1; and Hebrews 1. Think in terms of who Christ is in the world.

2. Discuss ways Christianity is different than other religions.

3. What do Christians in your country or denomination contribute to the global body of Christ?

4. How do you "go into all the world and preach the gospel to all creation"?

5. What does it mean to you to have a relationship with Christ?

Chapter 28: Leaving Calcutta

1. Read Jesus' prayer in John 17, and reflect on being in the world and not of it.

2. Describe any special experiences you have had when you knew the grace of God was moving you and surrounding you.

3. Describe biblical examples of people who had visions or other messages they knew were from God.

4. In what ways do you make room for hearing from God?

5. Describe times when you have had to reconsider things you thought you knew in the new light of your knowledge and experience of Christ.

Chapter 29: Finding Calcutta

1. Read and reflect on John 15:16.

2. Describe times of crisis that led you to understand more of your calling.

3. Describe the signs of a biblical character hearing God's call on their life and following it.

222

FINDING CALCUTTA

4. Do you have a Calcutta? Can you describe it?

5. How do the things that you grieve over reveal areas in which you are called to work?

Chapter 30: My Thoughts Are Not Your Thoughts

1. Read and reflect on Paul in Athens in Acts 17:16-34.

2. Have each person in the group study and share one worldview listed in *The Universe Next Door*.

3. Describe the worldviews Paul was confronting in Athens.

4. What worldviews do you confront most in your calling?

5. How do you describe your calling from the standpoints of your crises and grievings?

Epilogue: Fall More in Love with Jesus Every Day

1. Read and reflect on Matthew 22:37-39.

2. How can we increase our obedience to the first commandment of Christ?

3. What Bible verse contains great meaning and encouragement to you in growing closer to Jesus?

4. Are you currently "falling more in love with Jesus" every day?

5. Describe any struggle you may have or have had believing or understanding the incredible love God has for you.

About the Author

MARY POPLIN IS A PROFESSOR OF EDUCATION at Claremont
Graduate University in California, where she has taught since 1981.
She directed the teacher education program from 1985 to 1995 and
from 2000 to 2004. She also served as Dean of the School of Education from 2002 to 2004. She currently teaches doctoral students
and conducts research on the education of the poor. She received
her Ph.D. in education from the University of Texas in 1978.

Mary worked for two months with Mother Teresa and the Missionaries of Charity in Calcutta in 1996. She went to learn why the
Missionaries call their work with the poor "religious work" and
not "social work." This book of her experiences and reflections
reveals the principles around which Mother Teresa lived and how
different these are from many of those commonly understood in
the West. It is the tale of how this experience continues to shape
one university professor, and a tribute to Mother Teresa and the
Missionaries of Charity whose lives still speak to those who know
there is more to life than meets the eye.

VERITAS FORUM BOOKS
FROM INTERVARSITY PRESS

As a partnership between The Veritas Forum and InterVarsity Press, Veritas Forum Books connect the pursuit of knowledge with the deepest questions of life and truth. Established and emerging Christian thinkers grapple with challenging issues, offering academically rigorous and responsible scholarship that contributes to current and ongoing discussions in the university world. Veritas Forum Books are written in the spirit of genuine dialogue, addressing particular academic disciplines as well as topics of broad interest for the intellectually curious and inquiring. In embodying the values, purposes and mission of The Veritas Forum, Veritas Forum Books provide thoughtful, confessional Christian engagement with world-shaping ideas, making the case for an integrated Christian worldview and moving readers toward a clearer understanding of ultimate truth.